THE ART OF REVISIN

THE ART OF REVISING POETRY

21 U.S. POETS ON THEIR DRAFTS, CRAFT, AND PROCESS

Edited by
Charles Finn and Kim Stafford

BLOOMSBURY ACADEMIC
LONDON • NEW YORK • OXFORD • NEW DELHI • SYDNEY

BLOOMSBURY ACADEMIC
Bloomsbury Publishing Plc
50 Bedford Square, London, WC1B 3DP, UK
1385 Broadway, New York, NY 10018, USA
29 Earlsfort Terrace, Dublin 2, Ireland

BLOOMSBURY, BLOOMSBURY ACADEMIC and the Diana logo are trademarks
of Bloomsbury Publishing Plc

First published in Great Britain 2023
Reprinted 2023 (twice)

Cover design: Rebecca Heselton
Background image © paseven/ iStock

A catalogue record for this book is available from the British Library.

A catalog record for this book is available from the Library of Congress.

ISBN: HB: 978-1-3502-8925-3
       PB: 978-1-3502-8926-0
       ePDF: 978-1-3502-8927-7
       eBook: 978-1-3502-8928-4

Typeset by RefineCatch Limited, Bungay, Suffolk
Printed and bound in Great Britain

To find out more about our authors and books visit www.bloomsbury.com
and sign up for our newsletters.

For Joyce Tinanani Mphande-Finn
and
Perrin Kerns

CONTENTS

Contents

IMAGES

ACKNOWLEDGMENTS

Abayomi Animashaun
"Exodus" was originally published in *The Comstock Review* (Spring/Summer 2021), vol. 35, no. 1 (35th edition), p. 55.

Charles Finn
"Memory's Anvil" appeared in *Big Sky Journal* (Summer 2022).

CMarie Fuhrman
"Land Acknowledgement, Valley County, Idaho" first appeared in *Inlander*, October 7, 2021.

Tami Haaland
"Deer at Crazy Creek" appears in her volume, *What Does Not Return*. Sand Point, ID: Lost Horse Press, 2018.

Yona Harvey
"Hickory Street, New Orleans" was originally published online by the Academy of American Poets, Poem-a-Day project.

Jane Hirshfield
"Counting, New Year's Morning, What Powers Yet Remain to Me" first appeared on *Vox.com* and is included in the forthcoming *The Asking: New & Selected Poems* (NY: Knopf, 2023).

Rose McLarney
The poem "Given" contains many of the same phrases as "The Collectors of Local Minerals Are Likelier to Find What They Seek" and was published in the micro-chapbook "In the Gem Mine Capital of World" as a part of the *Inch* series from Bull City Press, Durham, NC, 2020.

Philip Metres
"Ashberries: Letters" first appeared in *New England Review*, vol. 22, no. 3 (Summer 2001), pp. 165–7 and was later reprinted in *Best American Poetry 2002*. It also appears in his collection *To See the Earth*, Cleveland State, 2008.

Shin Yu Pai
"Empty Zendo" appears in her volume *Virga*, Empty Bowl, August 2021.

Beth Piatote
"Because our Roots are in Rivers, Not Latin" first appeared in *Tiny Seed Literary Journal*, April 15, 2021.

Paulann Petersen
"A Furrier's Grandchild" appeared in *Birmingham Poetry Review*, no. 48 (Spring 2021), p. 141.

Sean Prentiss
"The Constellations of Slate Belt, Pennsylvania" appeared as "The Constellations of Slate Belt" in *Conversations Across Borders*, Web, 2012.

Prageeta Sharma
"The Witness" was first published in *The Opening Question,* Fence Magazine, 2004.

Kim Stafford
"Lost in Snow" appears in the volume *Singer Come From Afar*, Red Hen Press, 2021.

Shann Ray
"God of my abandonment" was published as the first in a cycle of three poems called "Montana Triptych" including "God of my abandonment", "God of my fear", and "God of my illness" in the literary journal *basalt: dark-colored, fine-grained*, vol. 15, no. 1, 2021.

Joe Wilkins
"My Son Asks for the Story About When We Were Birds" first appeared in *The Southern Review* (Winter 2015) and was reprinted in *When We Were Birds*, University of Arkansas Press, 2016.

Terry Tempest Williams
The passage "When Women Were Birds" appears in her volume *When Women Were Birds: Fifty Four Variations on Voice*, Sarah Crichton Books / Farrar, Straus and Giroux, 2012.

INTRODUCTION: WHAT DOES THE POEM WANT TO BE?

1.

What Can Revision Do?

There has long been a gap in the writing trade. Books written to serve writers offer strategies to fight writer's block, to enrich the creative imagination, and to seek publication—but offer little about how a work evolves through revision, how it gets clearer, stronger, and deeper, start to finish. This omission is particularly true with poetry. For all their brevity, poems must be the most highly crafted form of writing, often going through a staggering parade of revisions, while readers only see the wondrous result. The question remains: How does a poem travel from a first rush of inspiration to some finished, polished form? What was the poem's journey in between? How do poets take their first, often plodding drafts, and make them sing? What are the tricks of this trade?

The Art of Revision answers these questions, offering, in essence, a workshop in revising poems. By looking over the shoulders of 21 poets as they craft their poems, students, writers, and readers can see how poems grow, evolve, and find their final form. This book sets out to harvest revision lore, and to provide diverse ways to proceed in practice. By using real-world examples from working poets, showing side-by-side their first and final drafts, then letting the poets tell us why they made the changes they did, readers and writers of poetry look behind the scenes at the hidden pleasures of crafting poetry—and so can begin to gather a toolkit for their own secret practice of revision.

Of course, now and then a poem may flow freely from the mind to the page in some kind of magic perfection. But every poet in this book will admit that's exceptionally rare—a gift from the Muses. In most cases, a poem goes through any number of versions and can be literally years in the making. Coleridge was never able to revise to completion his incantatory "Kubla Khan." Walt Whitman rewrote his works throughout his life, from his first self-printed miracle book *Leaves of Grass* to the deathbed edition. Emily Dickinson's penciled drafts on saved envelopes are richly embroidered with changes.

But a whole book focusing on revision?

Revision in poetry is simple, is it not? After all, there are only three things you can do with a poem in draft: you can add something, you can take something out, or you can change the order. Granted, there can be a beauty in the first rush dashed off in a trance, but as our poets will tell you, when you start tinkering, things can get awkward, and your intuitive opening moves get muddied by calculation. Revision will be required to make the poem convey what can't be said—by using all the incantatory hints of image, pulse, voice, and shape. The fact is, the practice of revision offers something rare in life: the chance to go back and make it right. William Stafford used this principle in teaching writing, by inviting his students to "Think of something you did, but write what you might have done. Think of something you said—or didn't say—then write what you might have said." Revising poetry, by this approach, is a kind of salutary time machine: you get to go back to an important scene and have another take.

But in this process, tinkering through a draft, how do you make a poem better and not worse? How do you make it stronger without making it fall into some kind of literary artifice, some perfected form that leaves its original genius or potential essence in the dust? The 21 featured poets here will tell you.

When thinking about revision, we should remember that everywhere we turn we are surrounded by writing that has been revised, edited, proofread, and then released in finished form. Magazines, books, websites, performances—everywhere we experience the finished version. But we don't see the missteps and failed attempts. We don't see what was left on the cutting room floor.

In this book, 21 poets offer (1) the first draft of a poem as they put it down in their notebook, (2) the final version of that poem after reworking it, and (3) an essay discussing how and why the poem changed between drafts, how it was expanded, distilled, transformed, revised, and finally released from the labors of change. These poets share what they have learned from a lifetime of practice, their discovered habits of enhancing, cutting, enriching, and refining, and how might their lessons inform our own practice.

There's the old Mark Twain notion that the difference between the right word and the almost right word is the difference between lightning and a lightning bug. This can be illustrated concisely by comparing writers' drafts and final titles for novels. Toni Morrison wrote a novel she called "War," but it was published as *Paradise*. F. Scott Fitzgerald wrote "Trimalchio in West Egg," but published *The Great Gatsby*. Stephen Crane's "Private Fleming, His Various Battles" became *The Red Badge of Courage*. The same need for precision applies to the text of a work as well. In this search for essence, George Saunders has described speaking aloud to his draft, asking "How's it going?" First, he says, the draft often answers "Fine." "But really," Saunders insists, "how do you feel?" Then the draft may say, "I feel a little boring right here . . ." Then and there the work begins.

As for poets, Olga Broumas has talked about asking herself how a poem might be more like Proust . . . or like Faulkner . . . Woolf . . . Whitman . . . Dickinson . . . and finally more like Olga, a poem in her own voice. Jesse Herrera has advised eliminating the beginning and the end of a poem draft, and seeking the heat at the heart. Among the writers in this book, Jane Hirshfield keeps a page she calls "Questions to ask a poem when revising," which includes "Would saying less be stronger?" and "Does it allow strangeness?" Frank X Walker's personal "Revision checklist for poetry" includes "Are there cinematic moments?" and "Does it boomerang?"

As mentioned, the poets collected here will admit there can be a kind of genius in a first draft. The Beat poets used to say, "First thought, best thought," an approach that privileges the power of the unconscious to shake off literary artifice and trust what comes. But a corollary to this is a notion from the writer Reginald McKnight, who once told an audience that revision of any work should strive not to polish the text, but to make it more raw, primitive, even feral, working backward from the civilized to the elemental. If there is a kind of genius in the first draft—an intuitive, spontaneous, "out of nowhere" flow—we can learn to summon a second genius in revision, where that lively impulse of first discovery can be sustained. This notion of continuing creation can guide our experience of revision—it's an adventure unfolding, not a "final edit," not "polishing." The challenge of changing something good to something better is a kind of "happy problem." You are on the move as an artist, wrestling with treasure. Revision, when one engages with verve, can generate a feeling of luck. You cut something, and what remains gets bigger. You add something, and what was almost there deepens. You move something from the end to the beginning and the whole piece wakes up.

The task of revision can be looked at as the work of a farmer—cultivating young ideas and budding images, then nurturing the seedbed of first thought into ripe growth. If so, part of the trick is knowing when it's time to stop, to harvest, to call it good. For generations, writers have quoted the idea attributed to various poets: "a poem is never finished, only abandoned." Perhaps it's more accurate to say a poem needs not so much to be chilled to finality, but to be released to readers, to go forth like a child from home, to clear the writer's desk so new epiphanies will have a place to land.

In thinking about revision, it might be useful to consider a lesser-known companion word: *reversion*. Unlike *revision*, "to see again," *reversion* means, according to Merriam-Webster, "the process of returning; a return toward an ancestral type or condition; re-appearance of an ancestral character; a product of reversion: an organism with an atavistic character, a throwback." While *revision* of a poem can mean to see it in a new way—to make adjustments, to tinker, to watch the writing advance to a new form—*reversion* of a poem might be to experience the text getting older, more indigenous, more elemental. Like a salmon in home waters, the poem would go headlong toward the place of origin, shunning all impediments, distractions, or superficial concerns. To alter a piece of writing in this direction could mean to make it more wild, to substitute more adventurous words and strange effects, or to radically cut to essence.

It may also be helpful in thinking about the process of revising a poem to consider a kind of periodic table of possibilities: what, exactly, can one revise? What are the locations of opportunity for revision in a poem? Let's list them one by one: title, first line, lines, line breaks, rhythm, stanzas, words, word field, form/style/persona, the turn, last line, silence.

1. How could the poem's title be more intriguing, prophetic, indelible? It's been said the title of a poem holds about 20 percent of the poem's overall effect. How can a poet tinker until the title alone compels?

2. How could the poem's opening line be more arresting, intriguing, irresistible? Does it stake a claim, make an observation, pose a question, begin a memory? Does the first line appear somewhere down inside the poem's first draft, and in revision need to be moved to the top?

3. How could we revise until each line is more arresting, mysterious, leaning forward, leading on?

4. How could line breaks in the poem set up what follows? Denise Levertov said a line break represents "half a comma," making each line a kind of self-contained poetic sentence. How could we revise so the line breaks don't offer simply a breath pause, but suspense, implication, expectation, a resonant gap?

5. How could the poem's rhythm be the right drum beat, conversational saunter, incantatory spell? How could we revise a draft so the poem's rhythm quickens a reader's pulse?

6. How might stanzas clarify the poem's geography? If stanzas in a poem are like chapters in a story, how do they serve? If they are shapes on the page, how do they please? How might we revise so the negative space in stanza breaks is most active for the poem's intent?

7. How can the words in these lines and stanzas be the exact right set for this poem? Do they offer images, strong verbs, the right balance between exotic and familiar words? As we revise, which words are missing? Which words are in the way?

8. How can the "word field" of the poem stake out a territory? Are we in a dialect? Are we in the words of a child? Are we tasting words of sensation, hearing words in a distinctive soundscape? How could revision of individual words begin to develop the poem's own patois?

9. Does the poem present itself in some particular form? Is the poem a traditional haiku, sonnet, pantoum, villanelle, or a formal creative structure all your own? And how formal is the world of the poem? Are we speaking in a high, middle, or low style? Are we speaking some form of the "honeyed vernacular," a particular slant of enhanced plain style? Are we in poetry school, speaking "literature," or are we somewhere out in the untamed world? And are these words being delivered by a character or persona you have adopted as your lyric voice?

10. If the poem has a "turn," what species of surprise, shock, or transformation has us here in thrall? Where in the poem does the essential change occur—the deepening, the twist? In revision, how could we prepare for this turn, and then pull it off?

11. Does the poem's last line offer the reader some form of resolution—or oblique departure? Does the poem surrender to the urge to sum things up, to tame the moment with a conclusion? Or does the poem follow the advice of Stanley Kunitz: end with an image and don't explain?

12. How can revision engineer a particular quality of silence after the poem ends? How to cast a spell by shaping what was not said, what was implied? By this silence, what might the reader now suffer, see, know, or wonder? To this mansion of resonant silence, revision holds the key.

In addition to asking how you might revise, there's the question of when. Do you lean forward from drafting a poem and begin revision under the spell of first making? Or do you put it away and circle back later? Do you take a walk, like Wordsworth, to let the rhythm of your saunter inform the rhythm of making? Do you sleep on it, and rise renewed to see the poem in a different way? Might there be something to read, to investigate, after drafting but before revising—in order to seek names of creatures, places, tools, or other forms of textured detail to use in revision? Might you try writing in the morning, revising in the afternoon? This is the old notion of a cool head guiding a warm heart.

These are some of the considerations explored by the poets in this book. In some points they agree, and in others they diverge in delicious ways.

2.

How Does Revision Work?

21 Poets Consider the Curious Wonders of Revision

In this book the drafts show and the essays tell about the myriad ways revision works for 21 poets diverse in age, background, training, and style. You will see that their poems are widely various in form, voice, tone, and music, but in the essays describing their experience of revision there is considerable common ground, together with a wealth of idiosyncratic insights. A survey of their thoughts and approaches might touch on what they say about drafting, revising, how revising helps a poem get going, what the poem wants to be, shaping the poem, editing, getting help from others, the title, and how to end.

Drafting

Although this is a book about revision, many essays here touch on the kindling of the first draft. To begin, Abayo Animashaun reports, "I write in loosely held journals that are full of phrases, stick figures, and stray thoughts ... to see how best to shape seeds into poems." His routine, he says, is "when I show up each morning, I read a little. Rest in *unknowing*. Stare out the window, and idle in silence for a long time before finally putting pen to paper." CMarie Furman tells us that "I often think about the subject months, or sometimes my whole life; but it takes a trigger," and then "What comes, comes all at once."

Tami Haaland can report the resonant place her poem began: "The earliest lines came while I rested on a granite boulder split in half, maybe from lightning, maybe from millennia of freezing and thawing." And Joe Wilkins says of drafting, "I riffed, following the language where it led." Many here say the whole point is to surrender, to be immersed in making. The writer gets willingly caught by the lure of scribbling: "an eerie resonance pulsed through me as I copied a description of an ancient ritual into my journal" and "I gave myself over to a flood of memory" (Paulann Petersen); "My 'first draft' was a sprawling word tornado ... I liked the raucous elements of the draft, the winding, rambling sentences" (Yona Harvey). For many of the writers in this book, the experience of the first draft was visceral in a way that often must be partly dismantled and then reconstructed in revision. As Philip Metres says, "Sometimes the most elemental and primal feelings that bring us to write something—those radiant associations that are most clear—take the longest to clothe in words."

Revising

Turning to revision, our writers report ways to embrace the need for change. With revision, says Naomi Shihab Nye, "There's no reason to fear it or approach it with gloom." And Charles Finn reports that "Revision, in fact, is my favorite part of writing. The tinkering and changing, going over and over the same line again and again until the exact right word presents itself and the music of the poem is seamless." For Paulann Petersen, "Revision, too, is a gift from the Muse." A thought echoed by Jane Hirshfield: "Revision isn't some arduous 'fixing,' it's part of the making's original joy."

One of the primary lessons of this book is how revision can partake of the freedom of creation that brought forth the original draft, now a subsequent task in reductive change. As Terry Tempest Williams says, "The 'art of revision' is more than an outward tinkering of a particular sentence we often call a draft—it is an inward dissection of how we as writers come to a particular place on a page." And noting that the act of revision is closer to revelation than to maintenance, Shann Ray says that "[by] revising, my goal was to reveal, if obliquely, the unseen." The process is a kind of excavation, digging down through the first draft to find the foundational impulse behind the poem: "revision isn't about addition and subtraction, but lateral thinking and creation, taking the raw material of inspiration and passing it through the furnace of experience" (Charles Finn). And Kim Stafford says that "revision begins for me by asking the first draft, 'So what? So . . . this happened—why is that important? What's at stake . . . ?'"

How does this work, in practice? Jane Hirshfield offers that "The mind of revision scans in all directions, like a lighthouse: inner and outer, personal and impersonal, actual and imagined." By this roving scan, poets begin to see what must be done: "the idea of 'speaking to stone' disappears because it sounds too mystical" (Tami Haaland); "two simple words suddenly held expanded meaning" (Naomi Shihab Nye); "The word 'dizzy' entered the draft, then 'the dark hours,' then 'moon,' then 'dark wood.' I wanted a poem studded with sensations" (Kim Stafford); "I turn and twist the words and lines like a Rubik's cube until they fall into place" (Jimmy Santiago Baca). While this process is very personal, poets reach for common tools and make them their own. As Yona Harvey says, "I'll find myself quieting 'the rules' of revision I've heard over the years, which tend to revolve around the poem's neatness, conciseness, or some other kind of craft performance in the service of publication or external acceptance." As Charles Finn says of poems in this process, "I make them better by making them worse, and then a little better, and then a little worse, and then a little better. It's like rocking a car out of a snowbank." In this process the poem can change utterly, as Prageeta Sharma observes: "What do we do with the poem that changes so dramatically from the first draft to the final that it resembles almost nothing from the original?" Many poets answer: You follow.

How, in Revision, Does a Poem Get Going?

Many poets describe how a poem really starts to sing in revision, and how this gathering power guides the poem toward completion. This discovery can begin with a certain worthy disorientation, as Abayo Animashaun says: "I struggled. I couldn't hear the poem. It was unlike any I'd previously written." So you take small steps. "The first stanza had to be friendly," CMarie Furman says, but as she gets going, "Now the poem starts to chant." Sometimes there can be a "shazam!" moment in revision that sets the poem on its path. Yona Harvey reports, "When the poem was addressed to my ex-husband directly, everything fell into place." For Jane Hirshfield, the beginning of momentum comes when the poem "finds its question." And then, she reports, "Words become 'poem' ... when thought's slope and music start to steepen."

What Does the Poem Want to Be?

Throughout the revision process, many poets talk about seeking what the poem wants to be, as if the poem itself must become the teacher and the guide. Beth Piatote observes that "a writer is both responsible for craft (making intentional decisions) and for attunement to the organic form of the poem (allowing the poem to be what it wants)." She says, "I had to ... go somewhere with the poem where I wasn't in control of it but simply able to observe and learn from it ... to discover what the poem wants to be." "Give your whole self to the process," she says.

"I don't want to be sure of a poem's stance too soon and try to stay willing to be swayed," says Rose McLarney. Revision is the process of being willing to be swayed by how the poem begins to shape itself. In this light, Paulann Petersen questions "the seeming certainty of the poem in an initial version? This can be blinding. But revision offers to restore our sight." Philip Metres describes what this requires: "A poet needs to maintain two opposing sensibilities: tenacity and curiosity, stubbornness and tenderness." The tenacity and stubbornness are the poet's persistence to get it right, while the curiosity and tenderness are the means to follow as the poem seeks its final form.

Shaping the Poem

In shaping the final poem, some poets begin by establishing the structure, then attending to language: "With the poem constructed, the focus moved to heightening language" (Sean Prentiss). For others, the sequence is the opposite: "Early on, I'd found the language. I hadn't yet found the story ... And as I found the story, I found the form" (Joe Wilkins). Rose McLarney reports her fear of finding form too early: "The poetic problem that I usually resolve last is form ... if I see potential symmetry in a draft, I can become fixated."

For Jimmy Santiago Baca, there's a thrill in taking charge: "I read the poem aloud and whittle away a word here, a line there, then a stanza ... the poem's reality takes hold of me, and I become the architect." Sometimes the poet shakes up the form after wrestling with the original configuration: "I decided to depart radically from the original three-stanza form and ended up creating a poem of eleven stanzas, placed in two columns, side-by-side, like images on a cave wall" (Sean Prentiss). And sometimes the form upholds the poem's primary statement: "This is the beauty of subversion. Making the poem look like a legal document but sing like a poem" (CMarie Furman). Finally, the form and content of the poem may begin to speak to one another: "Organized by units of thought and pause between images, the poem is in conversation with itself" (Shin Yu Pai).

Editing

Some poets make a distinction between the substantive changes made in revision and a final edit. For Jimmy Santiago Baca, this stage can be radical: "I love editing, love taking from a line the few words I absolutely know are correct, and when I delete them I know I am screwing it all up. I love that sense of sinking forlorn, because it forces me to take a step closer to the abyss and look for new words." After plunging into this process, he begins the restoration: "My job then is to clear this mess up, to get at what I am trying to say." Joe Wilkins guides his fine-tuning with a set of questions: "Did I cut too much? Have I said all I needed to say? Did I say too much?" And for Abayo Animashaun, the revelation of the poem's final form can be a matter of a few deft strokes: "It felt clunky. False. But I knew I was close."

Getting Help from Others

Tami Haaland sets her private revision process in the context of a community of fellow writers: "The more comprehensive revision comes more slowly, less consciously, and often because readers—fellow writers and trusted collaborators—point out what I may have overlooked." Yona Harvey describes meeting someone at a reading who understood her poem's account of struggle: "We had a brief and beautiful exchange . . . and when I got home that night, I had a better sense of the poem's core." Even after a poem has been published, revision may be required, as Paulann Petersen reports: "after its publication, reading it to an audience, I suddenly heard the poem convey . . . another change." And sometimes the "other" needed for assistance is from the unconscious, as Beth Piatote suggests: "I needed to distill what the poem was really about, so I asked my dreams to help me . . . understand the soul of the poem."

The Title

In the process of revision, as the gist of the poem begins to clarify, it requires a title in keeping with that clarity. At this point, Joe Wilkins asks the fundamental question: "Does [the title] serve the poem? Has it begun the necessary communication with its audience?" Paulann Petersen expresses affection for her "little workhorse of a title. Unpretentious, but worthy." And Shin Yu Pai describes her journey toward decision: "Early versions of the title included 'The Empty Zendo,' 'For As Long As I Am Able,' and 'Pandemic Meditation.' As the poem evolved, I wanted to be less direct in stating facts. In the final version, I let the title 'Empty Zendo' do the work to set the tone."

How to End

The bookend to the magic sensation of starting a new poem is the search for a way to end. Joe Wilkins describes a simple ritual shared by many: "I read the poem aloud and listened closely for a cleaner exit." Once she achieves the essence of her poem, CMarie Furman finds the close: "The poem could not back down after this turn ... the last line had to carry the weight of history." Jane Hirshfield finds conclusion once the poem has achieved what she calls the "marriage of suffering and radiance." And for Shin Yu Pai, "The place where I decide to put down the pen and stop fussing with the poem is not the place that another poet, teacher, or scholar might choose to end. Ultimately, we find our own relationship to our voice and our objects through reading, practice, and deep listening. In this way, we are each our own teachers."

In the end, the process of revision itself becomes the school where poets most intimately learn their craft. As Naomi Shihab Nye says, "revision ... can be our best friend. It means you always have a chance."

3.

How Can the Process of Revision End?

Let's linger with this question of when to step away—a question that often comes up in the Q&A following a reading: "How do you know when to stop revising?" Is there a point where the music comes up, new light shines, there's an audible "click!" and you know the poem is done? Or do you finally give up, afraid you might wreck the poem if you keep tinkering? Someone (was it Horace?) advised putting your draft poem away for years, then taking another look. Ted Kooser says he revises until the poem feels like it was written by someone else—a stranger—and then he can tinker with abandon for finality. William Stafford once said he stops revising a poem when it no longer feels like an act of imagination: "I come to poetry for the experience of creation. If revision becomes just fixing something, I don't do it."

In a world of many indignities, revising poems may be a fundamental act of courtesy. George Saunders once said revision is like straightening up the house before a party—you want your guests to encounter what is beautiful and delicious, and not be distracted by debris. In the end, you want the poem to become a kind of rich and arresting crisis for a reader, something new and old at the same time, filled with language that feels lucky, clear, and memorable. To revise for this effect calls for a sustained and sustaining sense of play as we follow a series of drafts toward full awakening, rather than a chore of making stern mechanical repairs. We all need William Zinsser's motto: no pleasure for the writer, no pleasure for the reader.

A horse trainer named Ken Hunt once pointed out that when a horse learns a signal from a human being, it's like receiving a superpower: the horse can enter into a frightening moment, but by this signal can navigate that moment in safety. So it is with a poem well revised, a poem that has settled into signaling something beautiful and true. The reader has been given the power to live with a little more assurance and grace. In a life of grief, love, mystery—what greater gift?

SECTION I
"I RIFFED, FOLLOWING THE LANGUAGE WHERE IT LED"

CHAPTER 1
BEDTIME STORY
Joe Wilkins

13

First Draft:

At the Edge of Sleep My Son Asks for the Story About When We Were Birds

When we were birds,
we knew the wind & let it love us.

We veered & wheeled, we flapped & looped—
it's true, we flew. When we were birds,

we dined on tiny silver fish
& the watery hearts

of flowers. When we were birds,
we sometimes rose as high as we could go—

the light at such heights cold & strange—
& opened our beaked mouths

& let sundown pour
down our throats

& on into the very hollows of our bones.
When we were birds

we worshipped trees,
rivers, mountains, gizzard rocks, & like all

wise beasts & growing things
the mothering sun. We had many gods

when we were birds,
& each in her own way

was good to us, even the winter fog,
which found us huddling in salal or silk-tassel,

singing low, sweet songs & closing
our blood-rich eyes & sleeping,

wing to wing, the troubled sleep
of birds. Yes,

even when we were birds
we were sometimes troubled & tired,

sometimes sad, & so pretended
we were not birds

but stones, & fell, then,
like stones—

the earth hurtling up to meet us,
our trussed bones readying

to be shattered, our unusually large hearts
pounding—

yet at the last minute we would flap
& lift, & as we flew, shudderingly, away,

we promised one another
to never again

be so foolish. We told ourselves
we did it only to remember the grace

of wings, to remember
we were birds.

Final Draft:

My Son Asks for the Story About When We Were Birds

When we were birds,
we veered & wheeled, we flapped & looped—

it's true, we flew. When we were birds,
we dined on tiny silver fish
& the watery hearts
of flowers. When we were birds

we sistered the dragonfly,
brothered the night-wise bat,

& sometimes when we were birds

we rose as high as we could go—
light cold & strange—

& when we opened our beaked mouths
sundown poured like wine
down our throats.

When we were birds
we worshiped trees, rivers, mountains,

sage knots, rain, gizzard rocks, grub-shot dung piles,

& like all good beasts & wise green things
the mothering sun. We had many gods
when we were birds,

& each in her own way
was good to us, even winter fog,

which found us huddling
in salal or silk tassel,
singing low, sweet songs & closing
our blood-rich eyes & sleeping
the troubled sleep of birds. Yes,

even when we were birds
we were sometimes troubled & tired,

sad for no reason,

& so pretended we were not birds
& fell like stones—

the earth hurtling up to meet us,
our trussed bones readying
to be shattered, our unusually large hearts
pounding for nothing—

yet at the last minute we would flap
& lift & as we flew shudderingly away,

we told ourselves that this falling—

we would remember. We thought
we would always
be birds. We didn't know.

We didn't know
we could love one another

with such ferocity. That we should.

Finding the Language, Finding Story

Nine years ago, just weeks after moving cross-country and back home to Oregon, I was tucking my son into bed, and I asked what kind of story he wanted me to tell. In those days, my children's favorite bedtime stories were ones about when I was little, like them, and made bad choices. But that night, half-asleep, my son curled himself in his slim bed and said, "Tell me a story . . . a story about . . . tell me the story about when we were birds."

Whoa, I thought, holy shit. Now that's a story—that's a poem!

That night I tried to cobble together a bedtime story, and the next morning I sat down at my computer to write. While I keep a journal to house and hold images, observations of the day and ideas I'm mulling over, I do nearly all my actual writing on my laptop (and I close out all email programs and browsers, and definitely stay off social media during writing time—that stuff will be the death of you!).

I began with the phrase my son gave me—"When we were birds . . ."—and then I riffed, following the language where it led. I usually draft in couplets (you can't hide anything in couplets, all that white space forces you to interrogate every syllable), and with my children in mind the language turned immediately playful, full of rhyme and word music: "we flapped & looped— / it's true, we flew." Yet working with this fanciful, dreamy conceit, I knew, too, that to make myself believe what I was writing—to make readers believe—I had to be as specific and concrete as possible: when we were birds we "dined on tiny silver fish" and "worshiped [. . .] gizzard rocks," we huddled in "salal or silk tassel." We're not just describing the world as poets, we're attempting to remake the world, make new worlds. And that's what I was trying to do with this first draft: I was fashioning a sing-song-yet-hard-as-rocks world in which we were, and truly, birds.

The first turn—really, the only turn in the first draft—came when I read on Wikipedia (I do let myself poke around Wikipedia while I'm writing) that birds generally have large hearts for their sizes and that they sleep fitfully. After the playfulness, the world-building specificity, this was where something new entered—a bit of sadness, a bit of trouble. Which is necessary. The late Tony Hoagland once told me that even the most heartfelt love poem needs to have a seed of anger, that the most heart-wrenching elegy should be one part celebration, invective, or maybe interrogation.

Still, the first draft doesn't fully embrace that sadness. It doesn't let it play out to its logical extent, doesn't really get from *how* to *why*. The first draft simply comes full circle, which is a reasonable strategy for any number of poems—just not this poem. From this playful, dreamy perch my son had given me, I knew I had to go somewhere else. Early on, I'd found the language. I hadn't yet found the story.

And to be honest, I'm not sure how long it took me. I've written a few poems that arrived in days or weeks. There's a long poem in my third collection, one of two poems titled "Ragged Point Road" in *When We Were Birds*, that took me well over ten years to write.

Thinking on it now, I'm betting finding those last lines had to do with the upheaval of the move itself. My son was colicky as a baby—he didn't smile until he was nearly six months old—and even at three he was an intense, heart-on-his-sleeve kid, given to afternoon fits and sudden tears. While we had prepared our children for the move, it had still been hard. And what do you do, then, with a child's rage, with an innocent's despair—with the fact that we will all of us one day fall and never rise again?

I don't know anything to do but insist on love.

Which, day after day, is what we did with my son. Which is what I did, in the end, with this poem I wrote for him: "We didn't know. // We didn't know / we could love one another // with such ferocity. That we should."

And as I found the story, I found the form. The rigid, predictable couplets—it is not rigid, love, nor predictable!—gave way to a more associative, surprising, stop-and-go free-verse line and strophe strategy.

This is the only poem of my own that I've memorized, and on camping trips, relaxing along the river or sitting around the fire, my children often ask me to recite it. They are twelve and ten now, and the poem has become a family talisman, a marker for how far we've flown, how many times we've fallen—and that love is the how and the why, the language and the story, that stands us right back up.

CHAPTER 2
WHEN THOUGHT'S SLOPE STEEPENS
Jane Hirshfield

Country, New Year's Morning, what
Powers yet Remain to Me

I can make soup.
Can make, from last year's persimmons, a pudding.
Can climb a stepladder.
Change the bulbs in a track light.

The world asks — as it asks always —
and what can you do to change my deep-broken,
fractured —

I have no answer —

[   ]

1.1.21

First Draft:

Counting, New Year's Morning, What Powers Yet Remain to Me

I can make soup.
Can make, from last year's persimmons, a pudding.
Can climb a stepladder.
Change the bulb in a track light.

The world asks—as it asks always—
and what can you do to change the deep-broken,
                    fractured—

I have no answer—

[   ]

Final Draft:

Counting, New Year's Morning, What Powers Yet Remain To Me

The world asks, as it asks daily:
And what can you make, can you do, to change my deep-broken, fractured?

I count, this first day of another year, what remains.
I have a mountain, a kitchen, two hands.

Can admire with two eyes the mountain,
actual, recalcitrant, shuffling its pebbles, sheltering foxes and beetles.

Can make black-eyed peas and collards.
Can make, from last year's late-ripening persimmons, a pudding.
Can climb a stepladder, change the bulb in a track light.

For four years, I woke each day first to the mountain,
then to the question.

The feet of the new sufferings followed the feet of the old,
and still they surprised.

I brought salt, brought oil, to the question. Brought sweet tea,
brought postcards and stamps. For four years, each day, something.

Stone did not become apple. War did not become peace.
Yet joy still stays joy. Sequins stay sequins. Words still bespangle, bewilder.

Today, I woke without answer.

The day answers, unpockets a thought as though from a friend—

don't despair of this falling world, not yet   didn't it give you the asking

Stepladder, Vinegar, Persimmons

Each New Year's morning, I try to start the year by writing a poem. The first day of 2021, was, more even than most, a time for stocktaking, and what came first was a title: "Counting, New Year's Morning, What Powers Yet Remain to Me." The sentences that immediately followed it onto the page were factual, straightforward. I had, the night before made soup and persimmon pudding. I'd cleaned house, as I do every year-end, with stepladder and vinegar. But a list is not yet a poem, and though the title offered a clear invitation, the poem still needed to find its first-draft heart.

Leading up to that morning had been years of unfathomable fissure, unabating even in the face of a global pandemic. Each day, I'd wakened into awareness of climate crisis, extinctions, lands pillaged and waters poisoned; into the world's diminishments of diversity, resilience, and justice, its increase of heat, flood, drought, inequality, partisan divide. Each day, I'd taken some action, however futile. And so, the next lines came:

The world asks – as it asks always –
and what can you do to change my deep-broken, fractured—

The poem had now found its question, and so, its direction. Ink was becoming compass. But what then? Finding no way forward, I tried what one does, and wrote the truth: "*I have no answer—*" The line was impasse-admission, not Frost's stay against confusion, however momentary, that signals a genuine poem. I set down the two empty brackets that mean "more needed," added the date, and walked away. Time is revision's invisible partner I've learned to trust. It lets you see better what's there, and also what's not there yet, but could be. As in making bread, invisible yeasts arrive to work on lines left alone, in undisturbed silence.

Is it revising or "vising" to recognize when words are still a searching, not yet a discovery? A poem becomes draft as air does: when it begins moving. Words become "poem" when they start to carry some sense of news and of new destination, when thought's slope and music start to steepen. And so, to draw a distinction between a poem's "writing" and its "revising" feels to me without meaning. Writing itself is revision: each word, line, stanza revises what you know, who you are. Revision, in turn, isn't some arduous, afterward "fixing"; it's a way to step once more into making's original joy.

A person standing in front of a locked door has to do something. Returning to this poem-start the next day, I replaced *always* with *daily* – adamance rarely serves a poem well. I added some further countable presences: the mountain, my own eyes and hands, the beetles and foxes. Then, still hunting something I couldn't name, I moved the question up, to become the opening. With that, the poem's axis shifted. Its subject, direction, some sense of felt destination came into focus. My life was still part of the story, but was not, anymore, the poem's center. The world now was its focus, and the "I" in the poem became an "I" who serves.

Road markers matter, for the writer as much as the reader. With its ordering changed, the poem now needed a reminder of its subject and its dilemma:

For years, I woke each day first to the mountain,
then to the question.

This recollection of task somehow opened the poem to a larger seeing. A year turns, a decade, but what had actually changed? The line that next arrived moved beyond my own life, whether its powers or failures:

The feet of the new sufferings followed the feet of the old.

Pen paused again. The mind of revision scans in all directions, like a lighthouse: inner and outer, personal and impersonal, actual and imagined. It scans ideas, memories, feelings, looking for what might come next. The writer's job is to recognize what in all that to bring to the page. Because this poem began with questioning my own response to larger events, that realm beyond cooking and cleaning now needed naming. A transition line came:

I brought salt, brought oil, to the question.

The salt and oil and sweet tea are recognizably metaphorical. They hold many things the poem doesn't name—phone calls, donations, walking in protests, founding an ongoing project in conjunction with the first March for Science. The postcards and stamps in the line that follows are factual. I'd sent hundreds to prospective voters, congressional offices, government agencies.

The poem then stepped again into what had become its antiphonal mode, a voice and grammar more objective. What came were two short, declarative statements, one an image, the other, direct speech:

Stone did not become apple. War did not become peace.

Moving between first-person-subjective and objective, third-person statements is one way to summon larger perspective, though such craft-observations come only in retrospect. While writing, as Frank O'Hara famously said, you just go on your nerve, not on will or ideas. These new statements simply felt right. In music, in meaning, in saying, the poem had found traction. But transit is still not destination, and so, after another long pause, the word *Yet* arrived. "Yet" – in a poem, in the mind – is a gate. It asks you to think: "What else? What more?" With that word's assistance, I remembered something I've had to recall, with real difficulty, many times these last years: that in even the direst circumstance, beauty exists, and where beauty exists, it's a disrespect and rudeness not to see and praise it.

Yet joy still stays joy. Sequins stay sequins. Words still bespangle, bewilder.

The line took many forms before *sequins, bespangle, bewilder* arrived. I searched them by sound and by sense; the poem needed their insistent opulence and flash, their

25

slightly-shadowed gleaming. And at last, with the marriage of suffering and radiance come into awareness, the poem's original unsolved breaking-off point felt re-enterable. I wrote it again: *Today I woke without answer.* And this time, a next line came right away: *The day answers.*

For a writer, it can sometimes be as it was for the mythic Psyche, set her impossible tasks. What we cannot do with the powers of self alone, the world's insects, branches, and birds sometimes come to assist. In that final shift of stance from self to beyond-self, with the day now speaking what the day itself might know, this poem could go on to find its ending.

*

A postscript: At first, this poem ended differently. The line the day first spoke was a quote from a year-end email I'd received. I was happy with that: the poem had found its momentary stay, had done its work. It had revised me. But it felt wrong to borrow another's words for a poem that began with taking stock of my own capacities and pantry. I needed to find my own ending. It took days more, but the final line now is my own.

Is it odd to close a piece about revising a poem with a question of ethics? I think not. One part of revision, for me, is to test each poem with a series of mostly subliminal questions. "Does it fulfill its own music?" "Are the verb tenses, pronouns, right?" "Has it made some discovery?" Also: "Do I stand behind what it says?" "Is it ethical?" Ethics matter to me, to this poem, to a viable future. An ancient Sumerian proverb names what I'd felt was the problem: "You can't return borrowed bread." A poet's job is to be not borrower, but baker: to increase the sustenance available to us, in this world of shared lives, shared fates, and mysteriously assisting yeasts.

CHAPTER 3
INCREASING THE STAKES
CMarie Fuhrman

First Draft:

Land Acknowledgment, Valley County, Idaho

Let us pause for a moment to acknowledge the land on which this _____. This is traditional land

of the _____. They have stewarded this land before stewarding was a word. Let us take

A moment to acknowledge the way they are still removed from the land. Forcibly. Brutally. Let us

Acknowledge that soldiers of the United States shot low into teepees to kill the women in children. Let us

acknowledge that horses were shot that they may not be ridden. Let us acknowledge that Native people are buried all over this land without markers and that settler's graves are protected. Let us

Take a moment to acknowledge that this land was not stolen from the people

Whose language, culture, and religion is based on it, let us acknowledge that the people were stolen

From this land. The people who celebrate this land with song, with dance, with ceremony who do not apply economic commodification principals to trees and water and call it a resource. Here

we pause to acknowledge that the land you are on is rarely acknowledged

in these moments. That the land you are on is buried beneath layers of flooring, board and tile,

cement. Foundation.s. Let us acknowledge that the land that was once a garden

to grow that grew food now grows strip malls, amusement parks, stadiums and subdivisions--

let us acknowledge the land in the way subdividers do, with names like Forest Trails, and Big Meadows,

And Whitetail, which only exist in words which is how the government recognizes Native people

And how even our people have learned to acknowledge other Native people through paperwork and blood

Quantum. Today we want to acknowledge that these acknowledgements are written to nmake nonnatives

more comfortable, a check mark in another box, which requires only a checkmark and no other work

towards reparation. This acknowledgment is a paragrapgh long and acknowledges Native people with a glance,

sidelong, a moment in history the same way that Black and Latinx people are acknowledged. This statement

acknowledges the land in the same way that media acknowledges the _____ Native women
who are missing, this is not an acknowledgement in the way that media acknowledges one white woman
that goes missing on the land and for whom Nationwide searches are held and whose pictures is all over
our TV screens the way that ads with the faces of historical Native people are used

to sell a product. Let us take a moment and acknowledge the (animals that are no longer in this area/
extinct) and the salmon who can no longer reach their original homelands and the grizzly bear and wolves shot
for leaving (acknowledge) the territory they were imprisoned on (acknowledge) just like the (Tribes names
in the area) who were were shot when they left that land (Acknowledgment). Say their names. This land
acknowledgement was written for the people who acknowledge this land the way knapweed acknowledges it.
The way the blade of the bulldozer acknowledges it, the way the For Sale sign acknowledges it. This land
acknowledgement is not an apology. This is to acknowledge
that the land this statement is written on is the heartwood of a pine tree. This is to acknowledge that land
is being covered by water. That land is being burn. This ackowledges that when we step inside our homes

we can forget about what is happening on the land. Let us pause for a moment to acknowledge the land.
Let us pause for a moment and acknowlege that we can do better than a nod, a glance, a paragraph
that this acknowledgement needs to include action words like: join, assist, help, reduce, remember, learn.
This acknowledges that Land Back means languages back, means cluture back, means children back, means
This Akcnowledgement cannot land on deaf ears. This acknowledges that Native Scientists know the land
through stories *and* science. This acknowledges that Native People are still here and the land is still here
and that if we can take the time to write an ackowbwledment we might take the time to understand what it means.

This land acknowledgement is not an apology. Your land acknowledgement is trying to be an elegy.

Final Draft:

Land Acknowledgment, Valley County, Idaho

Let us pause for a moment and acknowledge the land on which we live. This is the traditional land of the Nimiipuu and Tukadeka. We should take another moment to acknowledge the ways Indigenous people have been/are being removed and erased from the land they've stewarded for over 16,000 years: Swiftly. Brutally. Culturally. Fatally. Let us acknowledge that soldiers for the United States killed women and children because they were Native. Let us acknowledge the recentness of this. Let us acknowledge the Native people buried in their land without markers while unnamed settlers rest in fenced graves. Let us acknowledge Indian graves dug up and looted. Let us acknowledge that place names like Squaw Meadows and Dead Indian *do not* honor ancestors. Let us take a moment and acknowledge that this land was not stolen from the people whose language, culture, and religion was born of it; let us acknowledge that the people were stolen from this land. The people who celebrate this land with song, dance, ceremony; people who do not commodify and commercialize trees and water or call it resource. Here we pause to acknowledge that the land itself is rarely acknowledged. The land buried beneath asphalt, concrete, floorboards, and foundations. Let us acknowledge that this buried land that once grew food and medicine now grows dollar stores and subdivisions. Let us acknowledge the land in the way subdividers do, with the blade of the bulldozer and with names like Forest Trails, Aspen Ridge, River Ranch, with words, the way the Government recognizes only Federally recognized tribes and has taught some Natives to recognize others only on paper, through blood quantum and CIB instead of commitment to rights and sovereignty. Let us recognize Land Acknowledgments that serve as consolation, another box checked on a list titled Due Diligences. The way wearing a Black Lives Matter t-shirt acknowledges white wokeness while the same whites shop at white lives businesses; acknowledgment as performative allyship. Let us acknowledge that internment camps were prisons. This Land Acknowledgement was written for the people who acknowledge land in the way spotted knapweed acknowledges it, the way a For Sale sign acknowledges it, the way the Forest Service acknowledges land by stating #itsallyours but meaning #itsnottheirs. This statement acknowledges the land in the same way the media and FBI acknowledge the over 2000 missing Native women and girls—by recognizing the one missing white woman for whom hundreds search and whose picture is present on all our screens, the way Native silhouettes are screened on paper to sell cigarettes. This Land Acknowledgment is inked on the heartwood of a pine that escaped the fires but fell for the mill from a land that cannot help but acknowledge climate crisis and carrying capacities, the grizzly bear fatally removed, and the salmon who can no longer reach their original homelands. This land acknowledges the wolves shot by stockmen and sportsmen to preserve the animals stockmen and sportsmen will thenceforth kill in the name of husbandry and sport. Let us acknowledge how we honor loss with dollars and not grief. Let us make depredation a science and pay officers from the bank of conservation. Let us acknowledge the words used to disassociate kill/er/ing/ed from the act of execution. This land acknowledges that it is recognized merely for its monetary value, recreational value, and aesthetic value. Because it *too* is living, this land recognizes us by our carbon footprint, our clear-cuts, our gold mines, and our greed. This acknowledges that Land Back means languages back, means medicine back, means ceremony back, means culture back, means reparations. Means *all* people depend on the land. Let us acknowledge that unless action is taken to identify and empower Indigenous peoples, erase inaccurate history from every school curriculum, carry out land-based justice and climate change policy, a Land Acknowledgment is a perfunctory, alienating, and otherwise hollow gesture. Acknowledgment means acceptance, admittance; acknowledgment is a dead word, is not a verb, is not deed, does not mean education. Acknowledgment means too late for an apology. Read me your Declaration of Change. Detail your Plan of Procedure. Show me your Map to Equality. And then, maybe then, I might be convinced that your Land Acknowledgment isn't merely another broken treaty.

Rhythm, Repetition, and the Drumbeat of Poetry

My poems begin in this way. I type my morning journal entry, tab over to the "poems" category, and begin. What comes, comes all at once. I write to where I feel the poem end. I often think about the subject months, or sometimes my whole life; but it takes a trigger, and for "Land Acknowledgment," it was simply the title.

I had a reading coming up in my hometown. I was asked to give a land acknowledgment. A request often made of Native people—backward in my thinking—Natives acknowledging being removed seems like a colonial way of being told not to forget our place.

I didn't agree to give the acknowledgment. Instead, I wondered, what an acknowledgment's purpose was, and who it served? What is the intended result? Why are they never about the land?

The following day, I typed "Land Acknowledgement" and wrote the first draft. Then I left it alone. Throughout the next day, the poem was on my mind. I went for a walk on public/treaty/endowment/threatened/Native land near McCall, Idaho, where I live. I brought my notebook and wrote a dozen more lines.

Two days later, I went back into the poem knowing the significant changes that had to occur. The poem needed a different form, a more muscular rhythm, and a tonal shift. The stakes had to be increased, and the last line had to carry the weight of history.

Lineated, the poem allowed too much white space. It had to have an absolute presence to create the first feeling of tension, of irony. I deleted the returns, justified the lines. Now it resembled a legal document, no more ragged edge.

Haruki Murakami writes, "... how did I learn to write? From listening to music. And what's the most important thing in writing? It's rhythm. No one's going to read what you write unless it's got rhythm. It has to have an inner rhythmic feel that propels the reader forward." This is never truer than in the prose poem. This is the beauty of subversion. Making the poem look like a legal document but sing like a poem. A stadium song of a poem.

I knew it had to begin early, and extended the repetition of consonants to embed the beat. "Forcibly. Brutally." In the first draft this made a nice end rhyme but didn't stick. "Swiftly. Brutally. Culturally. Fatally." Now the poem starts to chant.

And with repetition comes rhythm.

"Let us acknowledge ..." was crucial to the poem's tension. "Acknowledge and acknowledgment" are familiar words readers think they understand, but they are also grating, harsh words. They are a fist to the table, a stomp of the feet. Each syllable equally stressed. Repetition is generally incantatory, but in this case, expectancy becomes unsettling. Of the 715 words of the poem, forms of the word acknowledge are used thirty-eight times.

Because tone and rhythm are sistered, they had to be in sync. A song with a heavy drum beat is rarely about a sweet subject; thus, the reverse is true. This poem had to carry an authoritative tone—but not too soon.

The first stanza had to be friendly. I wanted to start with a warm tone, so I used the language of most land acknowledgments. I debated whether to make the poem specific to where I live, but this is a poem about honoring and this *is* Nimiipuu land. The further

I got in the poem, the more I realized that I had to have specific, current examples to keep the poem relevant, grounded, and relatable.

By the third line, even in the first draft, the tone changes. Acknowledgments don't address the myriad ways Native people have been/are still being removed/erased. Land acknowledgments tend to be gentle. Words like "stewarded" and "stolen" are acceptable. Still, stolen doesn't begin to reflect the horrific acts carried out by colonizers, and steward cannot explain the relationship Native people have with the land which does not assume human as superior. Steward also feels scientific, a Forest Service word. Repeated twice in ". . . stewarded before stewarding was a word," with its soft s and inaccuracy (both in description of the Land/Native relationship and the fact that the word has been around since *c.* 1300) it's removed. "Fatally" begins the shift.

"Today we want to acknowledge that these acknowledgements are written to make nonnatives more comfortable." Simply wasn't a strong line. The "show don't tell" adage proves itself here. So in revision, I honored what I was trying to say, but revised the feeling more clearly into, "Let us recognize Land Acknowledgments that serve as consolation, another box checked on a list titled Due Diligences. The way wearing a Black Lives Matter T-shirt acknowledges white wokeness while the same whites shop at white lives businesses; acknowledgment as performative allyship." The new declaratives are specific, clear, and have a little more bite.

The poem also had to express these acts in the present tense. NonNative America tends to think of Indians as historical. Yet another attempt at erasure. We are *still* fighting for the land, and Native people are still being stolen from the land. This is why, toward the middle of the poem, I had to show the imbalance of attention given to one missing white woman (at the time it was Gabby Petito) with Native women who go missing regularly—women whose names are not committed to National memory. To contrast this, I added how the romanticized, historical Native is remembered, "screened on paper to sell cigarettes."

The biggest failure of a contemporary land acknowledgment is inaction. It's almost an elegy. And though I liked the end of the first draft, it was too soft; it had to have consequences. The volta begins after, "Means all people depend on the land." A subtle but important turn. Not only does the reader have to acknowledge complicity, but they also must acknowledge that without change, we all face a similar demise. The colonizer can't win. The poem could not back down after this turn.

I revised the last line at least twenty times. I had to land the poem in a way that emphasized the irony of the land acknowledgment and what it lacked:

And then, maybe then (building up tension, also rhythm)

I might be convinced (here is the personal pronoun "I" for the first time)

that your Land Acknowledgment (the first "you," the two of us, the calling out, the challenge)

isn't merely (I fussed over that third word for hours. It had to be two syllables and carry the echo of "apology" and "equality," the *eee* sound that declares surprise or even disgust. It had to allude to pettiness) *another broken treaty*, a phrase most Americans know, and which is, of course, what is ultimately at stake.

It wasn't finished. After reading it to the audience in McCall, a gentleman pulled me aside and said, "I'm no poet ... just a working guy. But cement is powder. You mean concrete. In my job, using the right word matters."

It became "concrete," proof that it matters in my job, too.

CHAPTER 4
RESEARCHING THE MYSTERY
Jimmy Santiago Baca

Passage from First Draft:

River Run

. . . A quarter into my ride, to my left across the river,
others pray their mansions don't topple into the river,
red-tiled rooftops tier the hill,
Two rows of imperial hulls on the west slope,
buttressed with railroad ties, buried timber, laddered
to keep the ground intact, packed against crumbling,
pillared steel cross beams fortify the foundation,
keep the houses from crashing down—
floor to ceiling windows, tennis-courts
viga porches, patio sets, barbecue grills,
red chili ristras sway from beams, look down
on the river . . .

Passage from Third Draft:

River Run

Far in, high to my left, across the river to the west,
situated on the steep sandstone slope, mansions—
two hundred feet down, on a flat area a second row,
then the hill pours to the river where willows weep
and cottonwoods sulk.

Every year the cliff soil continues to deteriorate,
every year the erosion gets worse. Impossible
to stabilize or prevent flooding and still . . .
in two years of riding here, I've yet to see
a single person come out. The wealthy go to any length
to separate themselves from ordinary people.
Weapons scientists—Outsiders to New Mexico,
calculate drainage, rainfall, drought, mudslides,
certain their castles, teetering on the steep hill
won't topple into the river, a fleet of red-tiled roofs
lance the skyline, a banner of mock adobe houses,
imperial armada hulls that sail past interstate 1–40,
north to Montano rd.:
Despite the Russian olives and creosote shrubs
that run down to the second of row of houses,
the hill is too steep for a horse to come down,
even a dog would slip on the flaky dirt, roll
from the top deck all the way and kill itself
before it got to the second row of houses
where it's another shear drop to the river.
You see them everywhere—the rich
crowding in to live by water and beach.

Latticed wood and iron bars weave the ground,
buttressed with railroad ties, buried timber, laddered
to keep the soil dense, dirt packed against crumbling,
the hill fortified with iron pillars, keeps the castles
from crashing down—the occupants in their illusory
world of floor to ceiling window views, tennis-courts,
viga porch, patios, barbecue grills, red chili ristras sway,

> look down
> on the river
> baby,
> look down
> on the river . . .

What It Took to Get Here

I go to the river to blow the gaskets, gnarl the pistons, crush the rudder—after a morning of reading and writing I need to do something with myself—too old for the whiskey shots anymore, much too wise for coke lines, womanizing used to lower my after-writing juices, but all of that is the past. Now it's riding my bike along the river and running the foothills.

I do it for enjoyment, surprised as anyone when a poem comes. I don't go out to look for a poem. I go out to beat my ass down, to pray to Mother Earth to keep my shit together. I've got two kids still (five altogether) to put through college, so I don't have a lot of bullshit time—it's all business these days.

I think a lot on my ride. Sometimes without intent and for no particular reason, I'll see something and pull out my iPhone and record it. Before I know, I've got a dozen recordings of my impressions of the river or foothills.

I'm not really interested in the "I" stance, the posing in the poem as if I were important. I'm drawn to the nature of Nature, to her characteristic secrets, her revealing to me what's there that I haven't seen. If I stay long enough, and come out and endure the runs and rides long enough, something'll come to me. I don't do it for learning or revelation or anything like that. It's a natural progression that occurs, not purpose or plan or strategy.

And while I'm observing and voicing field notes, more for my own curiosity than any poetic venture, I'll get emails from fellow poets, ponder a bit, and include these in the overall field note logs, and make a real mess of my thoughts. My job then is to clear this mess up, to get at what I am trying to say.

In this passage I'm calling "River Run" from a longer poem, my initial writing of impressions is just that—initial. I drop in like a Paco de Lucía song, swirl in spirals immersed in my feelings. Then I cut and change and move observations around—lines, words, images—to set them in a more logical, linear fashion. During this incubation time, the poem is drawing me towards its needs, its desires, its wants—an umbilical tube runs from its fetal structure to my heart and mind giving oxygen and imagination. Here is where fiction dissolves and becomes reality, the more I strike and change certain words and images (weep . . . sulk . . . teetering . . . armada . . . creosote . . . kill) the more the poem's reality takes hold of me, and I become the architect.

I also found it important to describe the houses in a way that lures forth their imperial fascism, those houses that symbolize apartness, walls, us vs. them, division. The image of ships hearkens back to colonial days when Spain plundered indigenous lands and sent back that plunder on ships. I want to give the reader a foundation for what's happening, so geography and height and looking down are imperative. I include science and words that measure balance, collapse, and the breaking point. I don't like passive verbs, and I want to impart a sense of energy exchanges in the poem, enlivened interchanges. This place is ALIVE.

Writing is a mental health issue for me—it's my dry-drunk response to my craving for God's touch (the life-energy in all things). In the absence of that touch, poetry appears. It may not be God, but every word, I swear, is the burning bush in which I hear His voice. (I told you writing is a mental health issue.)

These words I write, these metaphors, nouns, and verbs all effect some action forward in my life. Poems both consume and liberate. When I write, I am no longer looking through the looking glass—I am inside it. Writing is cruel and unrelenting pain as you write to improve your lot. There's a sense that you've fallen behind, something is required of you, some entity desires your audience, that you missed something, that the living ahead entails you feel you have a right to happiness and you'll never really get it.

Poetry is the quarrel with Not-Having. There's our body, then our spirit. So it is with writing. Poetry: the spirit of everyday words.

I love editing, love taking from a line the few words I absolutely know are correct, and when I delete them I know I am screwing it all up. I love that sense of sinking forlorn, because it forces me to take a step closer to the abyss and look for new words. New Meanings. New connections. And after all, isn't that the purpose of spirited writing, to reveal, to feel awe (Whitman, Lorca, Borges, Bly)? To "engage the mystery, my friends. and get off your fat ass" is what they all say.

In this particular case along the river, I stopped and talked into my iPhone what I was feeling, thinking, seeing. There was a presentiment that something was going to happen with my words, so I flung the words out like nets into this little machine, and caught myself in them. I grubbed—this act of recording my words I call grubbing. I'm a grubber.

Unfortunately I run into others along the path, and it messes up my "catch," makes me self-conscious. But the act prepares my mind to be alert. Talk into your phone and you'll see. You shed your stagnation and it teaches you a lesson in the middle of the bosque to be aware. With your iPhone at the ready, you remain inclined to inquire.

This is one way to research the mystery in a culture that is very much on the go. By speaking into your recorder you remain pliable, you stay open, there's a sense of forgiveness about your small stature in all of this, and once humility absorbs you, it's a great place to write from.

Instead of being like so many negligible poets—spraying weedkiller, killing all the flowers—your spoken words give you life-cred (like street-cred). You're alive, you experience, you find yourself appearing on the playing field of life, fresh, ready, eager, trusting. On a bike or in your study, you are guided by the empathy of close examination. And whether you like it or not, this compels you to transform your pitiful adversity into inspiration, as if for a first time you see the beauty of your culture, people, and communal heritage, presented in a poem intact and in one piece.

This is as close as we get to touching God, the essence of what we've been trying to do in our work for a lifetime.

After all this happens, I read the poem aloud and whittle away a word here, a line there, then a stanza, working with a mind toward confluence and merging, a seamless sentiment. Using active words to give emotion to experience, I turn and twist the words and lines like a Rubik's cube until they fall into place, becoming an organic, authentic reflection . . . until the poem is tamed by the poet's surrender . . . until it is salvaged from the poet's *dreary obligation* (Joan Didion) into something beautiful, meaningful.

CHAPTER 5
CREATING A MORE BEAUTIFUL STORY
Sean Prentiss

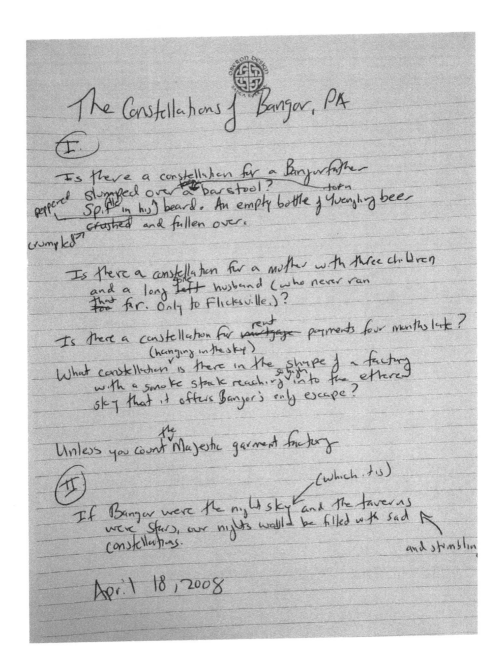

Intermediated Draft:

The Constellations of Slate Belt, Pennsylvania (with notes)

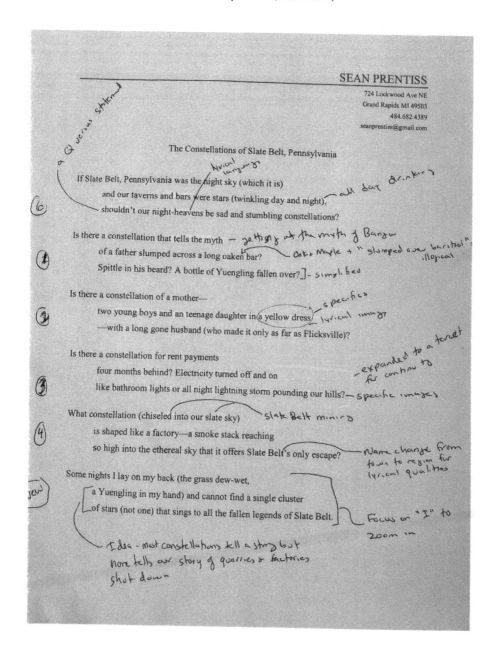

SEAN PRENTISS

724 Lockwood Ave NE
Grand Rapids MI 49503
484.682.4389
seanprentiss@gmail.com

The Constellations of Slate Belt, Pennsylvania

a Question statement

lyrical language?

⑥   If Slate Belt, Pennsylvania was the night sky (which it is)
     and our taverns and bars were stars (twinkling day and night), *— all day drinkers?*
     shouldn't our night-heavens be sad and stumbling constellations?

Is there a constellation that tells the myth *— getting at the myth of Bangor*
①   of a father slumped across a long oaken bar? *Oak + Maple + " slumped over barstool" illogical*
     Spittle in his beard? A bottle of Yuengling fallen over?] *— simplified*

Is there a constellation of a mother— *specifics*
②   two young boys and an teenage daughter in a yellow dress *lyrical image*
     —with a long gone husband (who made it only as far as Flicksville)?

Is there a constellation for rent payments
③   four months behind? Electricity turned off and on *— expanded to a tercet for continue to*
     like bathroom lights or all night lightning storm pounding our hills?*— specific images*

What constellation (chiseled into our slate sky) *Slate Belt mining*
④   is shaped like a factory—a smoke stack reaching
     so high into the ethereal sky that it offers Slate Belt's only escape? *— Name change from town to region for lyrical qualities*

new   Some nights I lay on my back (the grass dew-wet,
     a Yuengling in my hand) and cannot find a single cluster
     of stars (not one) that sings to all the fallen legends of Slate Belt. *Focus on "I" to zoom in*

— Idea - most constellations tell a story but
none tells our story of quarries or factories
shut down

Final Draft:

The Constellations of Slate Belt, Pennsylvania

If Slate Belt, Pennsylvania was the night sky (which it is)
and our taverns and bars were stars (twinkling day and night),
shouldn't our night-heavens be sad and stumbling constellations?

Is there a constellation that tells the myth
of a father slumped across a long oaken bar?
Spittle in his beard? A bottle of Yuengling fallen over?

Is there a constellation of a mother—
     two young boys and a teenage daughter in a yellow dress
—with a long-gone husband (who made it only as far as Flicksville)?

Is there a constellation for rent payments
four months behind? Electricity turned off and on
like an all-night lightning storm pounding our hills?

What constellation (chiseled into our slate sky)
is shaped like a factory—a smoke stack reaching
so high into the ethereal sky that it offers Slate Belt's only escape?

Some nights I lay on my back (the grass dew-wet,
a Yuengling in my hand) and cannot find a single cluster
of stars (not one) that sings to all the fallen legends of Slate Belt.

Without Myths or Constellations

As a narrative poet, when I draft a poem, I almost always have a story I long to tell, which means a first draft normally looks like a complete (albeit messy and clunky) poem. Slowly, draft by draft, I remove waste and failings and add poetic images and clearer ideas, moving from a sloppy first draft toward publication.

On April 18, 2008, I wrote "The Constellations of Slate Belt, Pennsylvania," a poem about how my blue-collar hometown feels forgotten by the larger world. Four revisions and many minor edits later, I had a poem I was willing to submit for publication.

The largest and one of the earliest revisions was moving the original draft's ending stanza to the beginning. Why do this? While this stanza worked as an ending, it more powerfully explored the poem's central idea that Slate Belt was a "sad and stumbling" town. By moving this stanza to the beginning, readers immediately had access to the main idea. This stanza also contextualized the next two stanzas, which speak about "a father slumped across a long oaken bar" and "a mother [...] with a long-gone husband." With the new opening stanza, readers now understood that the man and woman were from Slate Belt, a town filled with "taverns and bars."

With the original ending transformed into the beginning, much of the rest of the poem unfolded with each stanza bumped down. The problem was it now ended with a question, and while I appreciated this stanza:

What constellation (chiseled into our slate sky) / is shaped like a factory—a smoke stack reaching / so high into the ethereal sky that it offers Slate Belt's only escape?

I felt I was asking readers too much and offering too little by beginning and ending with questions. So, I searched for new ways to exit the poem.

The second major revision is the new final stanza where I introduced myself into the poem. This turning of the camera from Slate Belt to me, I hoped, would bridge the gap between me, someone who had abandoned Slate Belt, and those who remain. This inclusion of "I" felt vital because of my love and nostalgia for Slate Belt and my regret for abandoning home. This new ending also returned to the idea of how Slate Belt has no myths about those who toil away in factories and on corn and dairy farms, those who are un- or underemployed, and those who die from excesses. This ending provided a narrator intimately and explicitly longing for his town to be recognized.

Outside of reworking the opening and closing stanzas, I also removed the section headers because they served no real purpose. As for why I originally used them, the best I can come up with is that I was inspired by a now-forgotten poet who used section breaks. While originally useless, once the new ending had been added, the section breaks worked because they highlighted a here (I. of Slate Belt) and a there (II. where I "lay on my back"). Though the sections worked, I longed to wed those two physical spaces together because Slate Belt was and is a part of me, so I removed the sections and allowed the six tercets to become one unit.

Another round of revisions heightened regionality. I wanted readers to experience in eighteen lines my Slate Belt. In the second stanza, "oaken" was added to describe a bar as a nod to one of Slate Belt's many taverns, the Oak and Maple Bar. In stanza five, "chiseled" and "slate sky" were added to enhance the idea that Slate Belt was a town built on rock; its first industry was quarrying slate. "Yuengling" was repeatedly referenced since it was (and is) the beer so many of us drank. Finally, I changed "Bangor," which is my hometown's true name, to "Slate Belt" because the name of our region, the Slate Belt, lyrically captures who we are. We live in a belt—something that cinches and tightens—of slate.

Next, I heighten the poem's main idea. This poem was written about a town ignored because it offers little to the outer world. Slate Belt is a weary downtown, crumbling rock hills, and backroads winding through cornfields. Thirty taverns served Yuengling to its 6,000 residents. So, I added references that heighten the idea of Slate Belt not having constellations telling our tales. To get at this idea, I added "that tells the myth" to stanza two to connect with "sad and stumbling constellations." Later, the final stanza reminded readers that the narrator (a drunken me) "cannot find a single cluster of stars (not one) that sings to all the fallen legends of Slate Belt."

With the poem constructed, the focus moved to heightening language. I made a variety of edits, as seen in stanza one (see edits in bold).

*If Slate Belt, Pennsylvania, was the night sky (which it is) / and our taverns **and bars** were stars **(twinkling day and night),** / **shouldn't our night-heavens** be sad and stumbling constellations?*

In this case, "and bars" offered an internal rhyme with "were stars," while "(twinkling day and night)" highlighted the fact that Slate Belt residents drink throughout the day because they work any of three shifts, including overnight. Finally, the original ending offered a statement about how "our nights would be filled with sad and stumbling constellations." In the final draft, this line morphed into a question—"shouldn't our night-heavens be sad and stumbling constellations?"—to leave things open-ended. Finally, "night sky" transformed into "night-heavens" to focus on lyrical qualities.

Revision, for me, begins with a story I long to tell. I quickly create a first draft that lacks power, lyrical qualities, and/or a cohesive narrative. Slowly, I revise, removing each weakness, creating a more beautiful version of the story I first wrote, and working toward that original vision in my mind. In the end, I create some newer, hopefully even more beautiful, story.

SECTION II
"MY FIRST DRAFT WAS A WORD TORNADO"

CHAPTER 6
INHERITANCE
Frank X Walker

my body remembering
my mothers stroke
is all my headaches are

the anxiety i often feel
is just the weight of doubt
handcuffed to her hopes and dreams

my aching joints are call backs
to all the hardwood and porcelain
she scrubbed

on her hands and knees

i wear her guilt and sorrows.
every worry line and stomach knot
represents my inheritance
we dont stand on the shoulders
of those that came before us
we swim in the river of their fears

How much of our dis ease
will we pass on to our children?

How much of what eventually
took my mother
has already gotten its hands
on me?

First Draft:

In•her•it

My body remembering
my mother's stroke
is all my headaches are.

The anxiety I often feel
is just the weight of doubt
handcuffed to her hopes
and dreams.

My aching joints are call backs
to all the hardwood and porcelain
she scrubbed

on her hands and knees.

I wear her guilt and sorrows.
Every worry line and stomach
knot represents my inheritance.

We don't stand on the shoulders
of those that came before us.
We swim in the river of their fears.

How much of our dis ease
will we pass on to our children?

How much of what eventually took my mother
has already gotten it's hands on me?

Final Draft:

InHerit

My body remembering
my mother's stroke
is all my headaches are.

The anxiety I often feel
is just the tug of war between my doubt
and her hopes and dreams.

My aching joints call up
the floors and toilets she scrubbed
on hands and knees to feed us.

I inherited her shame, her guilt, her sorrow.
My every worry line and stomach knot
even sighs like her.

I don't just stand on the shoulders of she
who came before. Mama is my blood.
Will I drown in the river of her fears?

Revisions in Life and Poetry

As I approach both the age my mother was when she left this earth and the anniversary of her passing, I have found myself in a somber period. I can't help but contemplate what my siblings and I still consider her premature death from a series of unknown health complications. Often, I worry that the cancers that took so many aunts, my father, and eventually my sister, are an indication that my parents unknowingly passed something silent and deadly on to me that will ultimately lead to my own demise. This poem is born out of that space, and its writing and revising is, in many ways, emblematic of my preoccupation with those thoughts.

Maybe the same confrontation with one's own mortality eventually challenges every person of a certain age. Maybe it is something more. Asking hard and often unanswerable questions is regularly at the center of my work. So, I asked myself what invisible things did I inherit from my mother?

The writing process and my attempt to answer the question begins in my head. The revision process begins there, too, as I call up the words and phrases to articulate what I'm feeling, thinking, and seeing. My process includes a period of contemplation before I move to drafting on paper, then returning to the poem and initial question several times. I typically spend some time contemplating the seemingly unanswerable question and any and all images that mental exercise calls up. After that, I write, usually longhand in a journal, towards an answer with little attention to form or grammatical structure. I focus on trying to use words that evoke a specific emotional temperature and tone, verbs that move the action along, and any images that might capture a cinematic moment when possible. After I've gathered all I can in the initial burst, I type up a first draft so I can begin to revise on the page.

As soon as I squeezed out this rough draft and read it through, I recognized immediately that I had written past the end of the poem. I have a tendency, in early drafts, to unnecessarily continue to explain or attempt to make even more clear the main point, which might be advisable in an essay but is quite redundant in a short poem. So, I read the poem aloud and listened closely for a cleaner exit and an ending that felt like it clearly and more concisely made my point—or, as I say in my classroom, hopefully landed solidly on two feet like a gymnast at the end of a complicated tumbling routine. This step helped me find a more satisfying and less dogmatic ending three stanzas from the original end of the rough draft.

After recognizing how much of the poem was grounded in the body and the interior self, I removed the word "legion" which had the potentially unintended consequence of conjuring up soldiers and war imagery. I began a search for a word that would communicate a large number of things but still related to the body. The perfect word eluded me, so after poring over my thesaurus, I adjusted my criteria and considered "acres." Acres led me to "estates" and estates opened up a new possibility of imaging the domestic work my mother performed for wealthy families in order to keep food on our table.

On another pass through, focusing on the language choices I had made, I moved towards clarity by eliminating any unintended ambiguity and instances of redundancy. In a few stanzas, I made what I felt were stronger word choices. At least one stanza required a wholesale revision after my effort to articulate the anxiety I often feel, as a "fight" between two forces was not quite accurate. So, I considered "wrestling match" which still seemed a bit too active and finally settled on "tug of war" because I liked how it more clearly represented the tension which was an ever-present internal feeling but mostly invisible to others.

When I took a quick look back at the original draft, I could see that this latest one was almost half of the original length. I read over it again and asked, "Did I cut too much?" "Have I said all I needed to say?" "Did I say too much?"

Returning to the original premise of the poem, I asked if I had properly considered the inheritance I received from my mother and realized that the poem had drifted away from my mother to a more expansive set of forebearers in the last stanza. I considered backtracking and weaving in more details about my father and references to him and other ancestors in a more specific way, but I quickly understood that the original question was explicitly connected to my mother, so it made more sense to move in a direction closer to her.

Only after being comfortable with the contents of the poem do I focus on the shape of it. Even when I am not writing in a particular form, I still prefer that my free verse poems have an aesthetic that reveals a level of balance which occurs organically and not because of something I have forced on it. As I moved through the revisions, the poem seemed to lend itself to a series of tercets, each of which holds a nugget of the telling. Once I settled on the shape, I took another look to reconsider the placement and order of each stanza and even moved some of them around until I was satisfied that each was in its most effective place.

A poem's revision is incomplete if I haven't spent time considering the title. I don't ask myself if it's the right one, but rather if it fits. Does it serve the poem? Has it begun the necessary communication with its audience? I wanted to play with the word "her" that sits in the middle of inherit. Separating it out into syllables seemed like a good idea at first, but collapsing the syllables and just capitalizing the "H" provided the attention to the word I was seeking without giving the reader too much pause at the title.

One unexpected benefit of writing this poem is that it allowed me to inhabit a space filled with the energy and memories of my mother. I'm confident the time spent crafting and revising will help me with the healing process and allow me to offer this new work in her name. As much as I want to know definitively the absolute answer to the hard questions about my family, I instead ask myself questions about the poems that are born from my experience but leave me less paralyzed. "Did the poem do what it set out to do?" "Is it finished?" If it is, "how do I know?" What I've come to accept is that whether or not it is finished is an unfair if not a trick question. Like many of my peers, I skew towards being a perfectionist, but I have learned to trust the eyes and ears of a second reader. I now understand the truth is that my poem might not ever really be finished. Can it be made better? Possibly. Will it save the world? Does it have to? Are these the best words in their best order? I certainly hope so. Am I ready to let it go? I am.

CHAPTER 7
A MATTER OF INQUIRY
Rose McLarney

From the land comes corundum,
it's called that or a ruby. The mineral
is the same. It's just a difference of
grading. By an appraiser. He gets to say
what isn't a gem, what will be
a fortune.

And on the land a woman stays. The kind
familiar with hymns, and the one
who gave her as much of a life
as He did. Determining beginnings,
judging to the end. ~~She always~~
Always, she sings praise.

GIVEN
From the land comes, corundum,
called that or ruby.
The mineral is the same. It's just
a difference of grading.
By an appraiser. He gets to say
what isn't a gem, will be a fortune.
And on the land a woman stays,
sixth generation in the place,
sixty years a widow.
~~Familiar with hymns,~~ and the One
who gave her as much of a life
as He did, determining beginnings,
judging to the end.
Always, she sings praise.

First Draft:

Listen Here

From the land comes
corundum. Called that, or ruby.

The mineral is the same,
the difference just the grade

assigned by the appraiser.
He gets to say

what isn't a gem,
or will be a fortune.

Pearl, born and reared here,
who never strayed

far enough to get a look at the sea,
won't rise from the dirt of the place

again just because somebody
comes to her unlettered gravestone

with a head full of questions.
She can't answer them.

Except maybe as a voice
in hymns. To the One

who gave her as much of a life
as he did, determining beginnings,

judging to the end.
She didn't suppose there were other

tunes, words, for her to choose.
Always, she sang praise.

Final Draft:

The Collectors of Local Minerals Are Likelier to Find What They Seek

From the land comes corundum.
Called that, or ruby—

the mineral is the same.
The difference is the grade given

by an appraiser. He gets to say
what isn't a gem, will be a fortune.

A girl from this place
may be chosen

to play tinsel-haloed Mary
in the church pageant or

as another member of the choir.
To become the rhinestone-tiaraed

homecoming queen or
a wife whose roots grow out

from the platinum dye
while waiting on a man's return,

for him to remember the vows
he's bound to.

Why wouldn't she stay?
What would she do

but wear that dark crown
of hair the color intended for her?

She doesn't need to go off
after diamonds, or to study

some other distinction, knowing,
with certainty, there are plenty

of rocks in the dirt here.
She's familiar with hymns and He

who determines beginnings, judges
to the end. Always, she sings praise.

Identifying Gems

Early one morning, browsing a text on gemology and remembering ruby mining in the Cowee Mountains of western North Carolina where I'm from, I wrote the first notes towards a poem in my notebook. Shortly after, I went running and thought about novice miners surrendering finds to be identified and how little control people have over many situations. As soon as I returned, I wrote another entry—about faith. The following day, I copied the poem out in seven couplets with the addition of a brief middle line to bridge the parts.

For the next five years, the poem's opening and closing remained essentially unchanged, but I continued to re-envision its title and core. I tried to better imagine the widow's story in a version titled "Listen Here" to suggest her scolding a younger, uppity woman. I added descriptions of school girls, such as a child sitting on a grounded seesaw, unable to rise without the help of another body's weight. And I inserted a first-person speaker who could've been me. None of this material appears in the final poem, but I do file away my killed lines with the hope they can be resuscitated in future work.

Point of view wasn't the only uncertainty. My revision process is, overall, one of inquiry. I don't want to be sure of a poem's stance too soon and try to stay willing to be swayed. Even if the poem's characters have cultivated certainty in a belief system, writing about them I was wondering: Should this be a back-handed piece that uses the vocabulary of praise to critique rural women's possibilities? Or should I earnestly mourn a lost homeplace? I knew I'd been lucky to have educational opportunities, even if they took me away from where I grew up. And I knew that dislocation and loss of traditional place-based connections is a real tragedy, even if hardscrabble narratives of Appalachian locals are often romanticized (not acknowledging that they focus on the descendants of white colonizers, for instance). I decided I didn't need to be decisive and wouldn't include clear statements (such as the early line: "who gave her as much of a life as he did"). I'd let the poem linger in the conflicted tone of someone homesick trying to convince herself of the peaceful simple life of women who never left the region.

When revising, I also ask: Do I understand the material well enough to deserve to use it? Am I observing the subjects from a too-safe distance, or am I, via the speaker, at least equally exposed? Am I being self-centered to involve the "I" at all? The perspectives of the younger women were closer to my own so it seemed I had a better chance of portraying them with authenticity—and without the faux-folksiness I risked writing about the older woman. But it wasn't ultimately necessary for the poem to give space to an "I" to say what a person who moved elsewhere did or didn't find.

As much as I concern myself with big questions and meanings in my work, a poem's details require equal attention. So, at another level, I revise hoping to provide aesthetic pleasures that transcend difficult content or complete explanation. I'd stuck with those first and final lines not just because they established context and theme, but because of the musicality, color, and metaphors of their language. With the ambition of bringing these qualities to the rest of the poem, I identified specific strengths. The opening, "From the land comes corundum" (rather than the more likely phrasing, "Corundum comes from") is ordered so that the land—the source of everything that follows—appears first in the hierarchy of the syntax. The C sounds click with each other. "Gem" and "fortune" suggest values applied to more than minerals. In the closing, there are Hs alliterating, and the internal sounds of "always" and "praise" harmonizing.

Then I revisited possible poem-middles, concentrating on and conserving moments when the language sounded like music or real speech, and when it created coherence or complexity. In a version of the middle depicting similar scenes to the final poem but at greater length, I liked how "Wife" echoed "dye" and the down-to-earth diction of "plenty," "some other," and "dirt." Also, "crown," "platinum," "roots," and "intended" seemed to speak of more than hair, and the images of various ornaments worn on the head tied the stages of life together as previous combinations of imagery had not.

The poetic problem that I usually resolve last is form. I don't write in traditional forms such as villanelles, but if I see potential symmetry in a draft, I can become fixated. For quite a while, this poem was sections of five quintets each. To pare the middle down to those best features, I had to admit that I had added material just to fill out the pattern with even lines. But I did manage to find a new title in that material. And, no matter if, in the end, I must abandon a form, I still get ideas from attempting to adhere to it and the close examination involved in cuts, breaks, and making pieces fit. Creating the quintets had led to enjambments after "be chosen" and "what would she do," which I kept as I revised, to draw out the grander implications about destiny and helplessness in those phrases separate from the rest of the sentences. I returned the poem to couplets—its original shape—and finally it was finished.

At least, as a writer, I have an advantage over an artist who needs stuff as precious as gold leaf to complete her canvases or wields tools such as chisels that can irreparably fracture her sculptures—and over myself operating and making mistakes in other capacities in life. Writing, there are only the hours spent with a screen and at most some sheets of paper to be lost. And so many drafts can be made. And those, I can always go back to.

CHAPTER 8
GIFT FROM AN OLDER SELF
Naomi Shihab Nye

~~HOW~~ **BIG** *links lives* **Tears. Appropriate**

make longer + slimmer

ARABIC TAPES IN THE UNIVERSITY OF HAWAII BOOKSTORE

lilting tune

Yesterday our son came home from kindergarten
singing a ~~song~~ in Hawaiian, ~~lovely tune,~~
Good morning earth and sky. We tried to copy him
but ~~didn't~~ *couldn't* say it right.

Today ~~I face~~ the language of my ancestors
$14.95 in a 2-cassette box on the top shelf ∘
~~and~~ close my eyes, ~~falling~~ into the streets
of Cairo, Jerusalem, Ma'asalameh! Mar'haba!
~~the~~ clutter of tongues drifting, clicking,
~~the lilt,~~ the radiant wave! Nothing but memory
can save us. ~~Nothing speaks so deep,~~
shadow just below the surface of skin,
voice inside voice

I went to grandmother in stars poem

How big is gravity? Am I
bigger than gravity? he asked last night,
climbing the high slope
to our Hawaiian home.
~~you are not bigger.~~ *temporary*

Is it bigger than the moon
you can't put in your pocket?
Tell me, tell me!

~~And~~ *W*e stood looking out
over the valley   the fabulous
questionable glitter of Honolulu
~~that~~ we can't help finding beautiful
and the ~~big, big~~ *vast, giant, immense, stretching*
water beyond

to all our other lives
so far away

your small room with the red bed
my grandmother who will never wear a lei
~~the~~ stones of a village balanced
one upon another ~~/the link of our lives~~
and said
so big
I can't even say.

Final Draft:

Tears, Appropriate

Am I bigger than gravity? he asked,
dragging up the steep slope
to our temporary Hawaiian home

past wrapped parcels of rubbish and
ruffled tangerine trees and
everything else that did not see us.

Yes, I said, tugging him.
I mean,
No.

I wanted to be bigger than temporary.
Circulating seasons of wind
and rain, to hold vowels

close under a tongue till they dissolved.
Melodious names of streets become second nature,
maybe the song he sang about earth and sky

in beautiful Hawaiian language was also mine.
Is it bigger than the moon? It's huge. *Can you put it
in a pocket? Tell me!*

From a high rim over the city
lights/glass/traffic/construction cranes/
questionable glitter. Beyond that —

the blue that solved it all. Space
and waves making everything
temporary but true.

Always I ached for earlier times,
Robert Louis Stevenson writing
under a tree. Quietude of small pools,

two giant turtles sunning on a beach
without turning heads
to see us. In those days

before all the harder days to come,
his hair was long, he said, *Let's speak
only Hawaiian for the whole evening, okay?*

But he would have been
talking to
himself.

In those days he would still hold my hand
and thirty years later
when my mother was dying

we held hands again at her bedside as
gravity pinned us and breath slowed
to a halting wisp then fell. A shelf

of memories dropping forever
to the bottom of the sea.
O please! An island far from the fact of it.

The nurse acknowledged our behaviors
on a form, wrapped a white towel
beneath my mother's chin, and just like that,

gravity shifted — the one person you always
try to please, now gone. I wished you could
remember that song.

Gravity Changes

What a relief we may go back to things, memory forever unspooling, paper scraps and tattered notebooks offering their forgotten pleasures. How fortunate we may reconsider and reshuffle our thoughts until a line or phrase glimmers more than when we first wrote it—as if our older self is giving our newer self a gift.

So it wasn't long ago when I found myself in a closet upstairs in my family's 120-year-old Texas home, holding an old, incomplete draft of "How Big" nearly thirty years after first sketching it out.

The poem recalls the six months my husband and I spent in Honolulu when our son first attended kindergarten and all the questions he used to ask on our daily trudges uphill and down. Reading it again, I remembered finding myself breathless, trying to answer all the Why's, sometimes asking him to sing (the kindergarteners were studying Hawaiian language through daily songs and chanting) instead of talking so much. My incomplete scribblings were full of his voice.

Then one day in the University of Hawai'i bookstore, I saw some Arabic cassette tapes for sale and felt my usual shame that I do not speak Arabic. Growing up with an Arab father, I should have spoken it. He should have taught me.

This odd conjunction—Arabic tapes in the middle of the Pacific Ocean, while listening to Hawaiian—started the poem. It was the spark. But that early draft didn't go anywhere and I don't like ending anything with "I can't even say," which seems foolish and wrong. All we ever do is try to "say," so I put the drafts away.

Thirty years later, my mom was in hospice and I was at her bedside with the old draft of "How Big" I'd recently found in the attic tucked in my bag. Looking at it again, it struck me as something still alive.

When my mother died, the only signature required was after she actually stopped breathing. On that form, "Tears, Appropriate" was written by the nurse next to a question about our behaviors. My husband noticed it on our copy and mentioned it to me.

As in so many instances of a poetry-loving life, these two simple words suddenly held expanded meaning. Aren't tears always appropriate when moved or touched?

The "gravity" our son was once fond of discussing swooped back into the room. Where was mine now? When the last person who knew you all your life is gone, what ties you to earth? My shame at not learning Arabic would always be present, but hardly in the forefront. By now there were so many other shames! CUT, from the poem.

And how to weave in what I first tried to mention, of others elsewhere? The great poet Robert Bly, who died only a few days before my mother did, used to talk about "leaps" in a poem that lift its breath, expanding it to wider horizons. But sometimes, as I had often seen in my own distracted scribblings, the leaps need to be restrained. They don't help the whole. It's good to welcome them in a first draft though. The Robert Louis Stevenson reference then entered. He too had been temporary in Honolulu once. The Arabic-speaking grandma departed. She now had nothing to do with this poem. Robert Bly, I will always treasure you.

I hadn't held hands with our son for a long time. His hand was so big and strong now. In the poem, the hand now became a thread. His question about gravity rose to the first line. For the first time in a long time, I was adrift. An island of memories. Whereas the poem had once contained a bookstore, it now contained a hospice hospital room. Somehow, thirty years after the first draft, it also contained more of a life.

I simply do not see, have never seen, how people can live without writing things down. I suppose we all see our favorite activities as essential, but writing helps me stay stitched inside the body of our days in a way that I cannot fathom being without. And revision—which we might think of as *re-vision*—a new-vision—can be our best friend. It means you always have a chance. The random ingredients in the cupboard might still be mixed into a soup, a casserole, a poem.

I never think of revision as casting negative judgment on ourselves or our half-baked pieces. If you have to revise something for years, as many writers have done—this might indicate great care, not foolishness. And if your piece ends up surprising you entirely, teaching you something you didn't know before, combining elements in a way you never could have predicted—all the better. There's no reason to fear it or approach it with gloom.

My friend Roberto Bonazzi had an "ABC of editing": *Attention, Being, Cutting*. It might be a guide to living as well as writing. How much full attention are we paying to moments of today? Are we being present enough? What clutter of thinking or doing might we trim away? All these questions hold true when revising a poem.

CHAPTER 9
A POEM'S TRUEST EXPRESSION

Yona Harvey

it's hard to settle on a place to settle
on a life when it seems the only life
we know is restlessness that strange
home where no one knocks on the
door before entering a room and yells
if the door is locked and misunderstands
if the door is closed is home a circle
a loop a curve of constant grievances
that play out, sister to sister or
brother to brother or eldest to
youngest or granny's favorite with
the twenty dollar bill in her
christmas stocking when the others
get laced dressed dollies with long
lashes curved above the eyes that
blink above it all but never tell
what passes across the home table
the home spoons the home knives
too dull to cut but angular
enough to make you think to
twice about home

the last thing i said was maybe let's
buy a duplex like you live on your
side and i'll live on my side and
you'll rise when you rise and i'll rise
when i rise and place my sensible

First Draft:

Hickory Street, New Orleans

mother daughter granddaughter rebel nursing major mouse bully bullied
burger flipper country countryfied wife burger dresser girlfriend secretary
city-fied teacher taunter teaser cashier poet patron put-upon student
editor irritated wonder woman

it's hard to settle on a place to settle on a life when it seems the only life we know is
restlessness, that strange home where no one knocks on the door before entering a room
and yells if the door is locked and misunderstands if the door is closed is home a circle a
loop a curve of constant grievances that play out sister to sister or brother to brother or
eldest to youngest or granny's favorite with the twenty dollar bill in her Christmas
stocking when the others get laced dresses dollies with long lashes curved above the eyes
that blink above it all but never tell what passes across the home table the home spoons
the home knives too dull to cut but angular enough to make you think twice about home
the last thing i said was maybe let's buy a duplex, like you live on your side and i'll live on
my side and you'll rise when you rise and i'll rise when i rise and place my sensible shoes
near the back porch door and plant tall grasses and blooms in a border design and worry
little about too early winter and confused birds in early formation and dying bees and
ladybug shortages and you'll worry little about slow-dancing couples on talent show
programs with B actors and minor celebrities or whatever happened to sarah palin and
the gang all pit bulls with lipstick and the sideshow before the current sideshow and the
faux chrisian values and tutus and sparkling stockings and tap dancing shoes for sale i
said something like let's divide these hurts and regrets and you get a pile and I get a pile
and you walk a block and i'll walk a block and you get a pug and i get a poodle and you
stub a toe and i crack an elbow and you get citizenship and i get a green card or you
interrupt and i intercept and you call a friend and i call the mayor and you sing the blues
and i scratch a record or maybe seal off all sound in a bomb shelter sheltering the
shuddering of the heart the swell of the chest the high-pitched operas of feral cats beyond
the last bus stop at the edge of the neighborhood where the woods meet the long stretches
of uncut grass where no one's quite sure who owns the land though everyone's certain the
land's not for sale and what's the word for that wealthy healthy feeling like nonsense from
a romance novel and a bungalow near the beach that's never quite specified but walked
upon by lovers barefoot and ocean kissed and maybe mesmerized by the sudden drift of
a giant sea turtle floating toward a green wave darkened with midnight and somehow
they're safe, the couple is safe and there's no stilts that will break, no stars that will bend,
there's just miles and miles of ocean and the benefits of salt on the tongue and hair and
the slow belief in certain days of the week that all blend together for the sake of this story,
this fair-weather sky, this dreamlike bouquet of

Final Draft:

Hickory Street, New Orleans

Like, the last thing I said to you was let's buy a duplex,
like, you live on your side & I'll live on my side &
you'll rise when you rise & I'll rise when I rise &
I said something like, let's divide these hurts & regrets
& you get a stack & I get a stack & you walk a block
& I walk a block & you get a poodle & I get a pug
& you stub a toe & I twist an ankle & you get
a wheelbarrow & I get chickens glazed with rain

& you interrupt & I intercept & you call
the Congressman & I call the Mayor & you bruise
a trumpet & I smash a tuba or maybe seal off all sound

sheltering the shuddering of the heart compressed

the high-pitched operas of trolley wheels breaking
at the edge of midnight where magnolias
shelter the stoplights & left-footed lovers, drunk
on beignets & champagne-kisses & maybe struck
by the distant drift of a giant
sea turtle floating toward a green wave
in a tacky, overpriced painting
& somehow they're safe, the couple is safe
& there's no parade stilts that will break, no stars
that will bend, there's just an orchid
tucked behind an ear & hours blurred together &

you said—

& I said—

Remember?

True Expression as the Last Trolley Stop

"Hickory Street, New Orleans" began in my writing group. In this group members take turns reading and then leading a sequence of generative prompts. We usually include a word bank from which we can choose three to four words or phrases designed to jolt us out of our typical writing habits or choices. When it was my turn to lead, I asked everyone to make a list of the roles they've held or personas they've adopted over the years and write a run-on sentence about home. I then had everyone write for twenty-five more minutes using the material generated from the short prompts.

My first draft was a sprawling word tornado, a list of occupations and personas several words long. It included, "mother," "grandmother," "nursing major," "burger flipper," and "wonder woman." The next part of the assignment ran four more pages. Typically, these drafts remain in my notebook for three or four weeks before I type them, but there was a Mardi Gras event coming up in Pittsburgh I was invited to read at and I thought my notebook draft might work—I liked the raucous elements of the draft, the winding, rambling sentences, and the lines about music. I knew, too, I could experiment with the sound and feel of the poem and make additional changes later, that it didn't need to be perfect. After that reading, a woman approached me and reticently mentioned that she was going through a divorce. I'd been through one a few years ago. We had a brief and beautiful exchange about those difficulties and when I got home that night, I had a better sense of the poem's core.

In the coming weeks, I deleted the section about my grandmother and the Christmas stockings, which no longer felt important. I also noticed that "the last thing I said" in the notebook had become "the last thing I said to him" in a version I titled "Mardi Gras Poem with a Nod to Home." But when I was alone again with the poem, I felt "the last thing I said to *you*" was the truest iteration. When the poem was addressed to my ex-husband directly, everything fell into place. I used the opening word "Like" because it felt more intimate and sonically conveyed the speaker's discomfort and reluctance. And because the poem was now addressed to a person I could see as opposed to an abstract stand-in, I generated lines about the "wheelbarrow" and "chickens glazed with rain," a playful wink at the image of two poets separating rather than a generic couple.

Addressing the poem to "you" also helped me visualize a specific setting. Hickory Street is close to the start of the trolley route that goes from Uptown New Orleans to the French Quarter. By setting the poem there, I decided I could suggest Mardi Gras rather than have it be explicit. I also liked the idea of ending on quietude and a shared memory rather than the brouhaha of arguing that sets the poem in motion. In earlier versions, I kept what the speaker "said" in the company of an outrageous catalog of American spectacle: "Sarah Palin & the gang," "sideshows," "faux Christian values & tutus & sparkling stockings," and so on. But I realized these tangents were no longer needed—nor the references to climate change ("too early winter & confused birds / in early formation & dying bees & ladybug shortages") and gentrification ("where no one's quite sure who owns the lot / though everyone's sure the land's not for sale"), which I could reserve for future poems.

I eventually added the long pauses at the end by using dashes. I frequently use dashes in my poems as markers of hesitation, of interruption, of what I call ongoingness. As far as I'm concerned, life keeps moving, going on. I also wanted to capture the sentiment that when it comes to divorce or other challenging relationship changes, when moving forward it ultimately doesn't matter much what anyone says. I think of revision in a similar light. I'll find myself quieting "the rules" of revision I've heard over the years, which tend to revolve around the poem's neatness, conciseness, or some other kind of craft performance in the service of publication or external acceptance. Instead of hyper-focusing on punctuation or other details that will eventually be corrected, however, I think more deeply about the poem's truest expressions. Making this choice has more to do with maturity and necessity than talent—both of which I've grown to covet in recent years. I ask myself if the version before me is closest to what the poem needs to say. If the answer is yes, then I know the poem is done.

CHAPTER 10
AN INWARD DISSECTION
Terry Tempest Williams

Original Prose Paragraph:

When Women Were Birds

Once upon a time, when women were birds, there was the simple understanding that to sing at dawn and to sing at dusk was to heal the world through joy. The birds still remember what we have forgotten, that the world is meant to be celebrated.

When Women Were Birds

Once upon a time, when women were birds
there was the simple understanding that
to sing at dawn and to sing at dusk
was to heal the world through joy.
The birds still remember
what we have forgotten
that the world
is meant to be
celebrated.

Once Upon a Time

Now is the time to tell the truth—to be a sleuth to our sources—to uncover the origin stories of our published words that emerge perfectly positioned, polished, and untethered to their history. The "art of revision" is more than an outward tinkering of a particular sentence we often call a draft—it is an inward dissection of how we as writers come to a particular place on a page and write the end point of a question brought to the surface of a poem or a passage conscious or unconscious of its arrival.

Once upon a time, when women were birds, there was the simple understanding that to sing at dawn and to sing at dusk was to heal the world through joy. The birds still remember what we have forgotten, that the world is meant to be celebrated.

This is the passage I will choose to ground truth from *When Women Were Birds*, a book about how one finds one's voice. It is the last paragraph of the book, the epilogue withstanding. Here it is reimagined with line breaks as it was later imagined as a poem:

> *Once upon a time, when women were birds*
> *there was the simple understanding that*
> *to sing at dawn and to sing at dusk*
> *was to heal the world through joy.*
> *The birds still remember*
> *what we have forgotten*
> *that the world*
> *is meant to be*
> *celebrated.*

Before my mother, Diane Dixon Tempest died from ovarian cancer in the winter of 1987, she told me that she was leaving me all her journals. I did not know my mother kept journals. This was a revelation to me. Her instructions were simple: "But you must not look at them until after I am gone." She passed one week later. One month later, I found her journals exactly where she said they would be—in a closet, three shelves full. I opened the first journal. It was empty. I opened the second journal, it was empty. I opened the third, the fourth, the fifth, and the sixth journal—all of them empty. Shelf after shelf after shelf, all of my mother's journals were blank.

It was as though my mother died twice. I held this painful and curious fact, this story inside of me for over twenty years.

Why? Why had my mother left me her blank journals? This was the question that fueled my writing in *When Women Were Birds: 54 Variations on Voice* for decades. The women told me they had no voice—that they were incarcerated by fear and loneliness. What needs to be counted on to have a voice? Courage. Anger. Love. Something to say; someone to speak to; someone to listen?

The title came before the book. I thought it came to me in a dream. What came before the title is what interested me in thinking about what led me to write and possibly revise this last passage/poem in *When Women Were Birds*. I went back into my files and correspondences.

What I found was this excerpt from a letter to my friend Alexandra Fuller:

Dearest Bo:

I spent a day and a night and a day in the Soda Springs Jail on Sunday, after driving home from the funeral in Salt Lake City. The charge: driving 48 mph in a 35 mph zone with a suspended license, that I didn't know about, for forgetting to pay for a traffic ticket in June—5 mph over the speed limit in my father's neighborhood before leaving for Maine.

With flashing red lights in my rear view mirror and the sound of a siren, a policeman named Deputy Green pulled me over. I was driving from Salt Lake to Jackson, Wyoming, after attending the funeral of my niece's daughter barely a week old, dead from cancer. My mind was elsewhere. I couldn't find my car registration. The cop returned to his car with my driver's license for what seemed like forever. I found the piece of paper I was looking for and made the mistake of getting out of my car and handing him my registration. The next thing I know I am leaning against the back of my car with a pistol in the small of my back. I am told to spread my legs and put my hands up. The officer then yells at me, "What else aren't you telling me?"

... I could not speak. My voice left me ... I was fingerprinted and booked, quickly taken into a women's block of inmates. What I learned was immense in the time spent, shared, and lived with twelve young Mormon mothers addicted to meth.

... Shattered. I'm still there with these women mentally and emotionally, haunted by their stories, their lives, their goodness. Still seeing them lying on their stainless steel bunks with one thin sheet and a dirty wool blanket, curled in fetal positions, facing the wall, the white cinderblock wall, with one toilet, one shower, one sink, and four circular steel tables bolted down with attached stools. The mirror that is a window. If I ever thought for one moment, I was someone different, all I had to do was look in the mirror, orange and white stripes, locked down, locked in. A prisoner. All of us.

... We are all in pain. We carry our personal histories, traumas, and biases with us. How do we use our power? Who has a voice and how do we use it? We are all in search of purpose and being of use. Even in jail, these women spoke of their remembered joys: their children; a river trip down the Colorado; the Yellowstone; a love of a good book; music; a quilt waiting to be finished; a fresh, ripe apple; and how they were just trying to catch up with the demands of their lives and got caught short when they were desperate or looking for a little help and relief.

We have all been there. I am there now. Speed comes in many forms.

What became clear to me in the Caribou County Jail in those thirty-six hours was this: After listening to these women's stories, what we have in common, regardless of our differences, is a voice. What we also share as women is how quickly we lose our voices through our fears when confronted by the patriarchy in all its manifestations. Once upon a time when women were birds—this was not the case.

My love,
Terry

Reading this letter, looking back on that experience in Soda Springs, Idaho, what I remember alongside the women's voices inside the jail were the birds singing outside at dusk and dawn. Five years later, that image unconsciously appeared in that final paragraph, now a poem. This was not a revision, but a private revelation lost and found, revisited.

SECTION III
"IT FELT CLUNKY, FALSE, BUT I KNEW I WAS CLOSE"

CHAPTER 11
TO SEE AGAIN
Paulann Petersen

THURSDAY
SEPTEMBER 21

TOWEL —
someone "pulled through the
flayed skin of a sacrificed
animal as a sign of death
and rebirth")

Once
As soon as I could walk,
my grandfather made me
a fur coat and matching hat.
White cony. In the snapshot,
I'm a toddler smile with fat cheeks
to each side, plump legs escaping
from the coat's bottom hem
to finish in lace-trimmed anklets
and patent leather mary janes.
My grandmother would have made
the lining for that coat. White satin
to lie between the skin's pelt's soft
underside and my skin. In a year I
would outgrow that coat. But there
would be others. Hundreds I tried on
in the fur shop, their length dragging
the floor, their sleeves consuming
my wrists and hands

Each time I crawled into the animal's
skin I could feel its death the
soft beauty of its death. I stroked
the terror of its beauty each time
the animal me slip it off
my shoulders, I was reborn

Intermediate Draft:

A Furrier's Grandchild

SACRIFIC~~IAL~~ *AL*

Once I took ~~my~~ *a* first step,
my grandfather made me
a fur coat and matching hat.
White cony. In a snapshot,
I'm ~~a~~ *around* toddler-smile with ~~fat~~ cheeks
to each side, plump legs that escape
from the coat's bottom edge
to ~~finish~~ *end* inside lace-trimmed anklets
and patent leather Mary Janes.

My grandmother made the lining
for that coat. White satin to lie
between the pelt's napped underside
/ and my skin. In a year,
I would /outgrow that cony coat./
But there would be others, each
just my size. And the hundreds—
women's coats—I tried on *later*
in front of the fur shop's
triptych of mirror. Their length   ~~mirror~~ *triptych mirror.*
dragged the floor, their sleeves
overtaking my wrists and hands.

Each time I crawled into
~~an~~ animal's skin, I could feel
the soft clutch of its death.
Cool. Sleek. Gleaming. I stroked
that terrible beauty. Each time
the animal let me peel itself
off my shoulders, lift its weight
to hang from the cold metal rack,
I was reborn.

off my shoulders let me
return its weight to hang
from the cold metal rack,
I was reborn.

off my shoulders, let me
return the fall of its weight
to the garment rack's ~~metal~~,
I was reborn.   *steel*

to the ~~hook~~ steel garment rack,

the fall of its weight
return its changing weight
to the cold metal rack
rack's cold metal,
I was reborn.

Final Draft:

A Furrier's Grandchild

Once I'd taken my first step,
my grandfather made me
a fur coat and matching hat.
White cony. My grandmother made
the lining. Pale satin to lie
between the pelt's napped underside
and my skin. In a year, I would
outgrow that cony coat.
But there would be others, each
just my ascended size. And hundreds
of customers' coats—the chinchilla,
mink, and Persian lamb
I later tried on
in front of the fur shop's
triptych mirror. Their length
dragging the floor, their sleeves
overtaking my wrists and hands.

Each time I entered
an animal's skin, I could feel
the soft clutch of its death.
Cool. Sleek. Gleaming.
                          I stroked
                 that terrible beauty.
Each time the animal let me peel it
away from my shoulders, let me
return its fallen weight to hang
from the rack's cold steel bar,
I emerged. Reborn.

I Hear the Poem Speak For Itself

Sitting out on my deck in early fall warmth, an eerie resonance pulsed through me as I copied a description of an ancient ritual into my journal—a rite that included being "pulled through the flayed skin of a sacrificial animal as a sign of death and rebirth." Both stunned and jolted, I gave myself over to a flood of memory: me, a furrier's only grandchild, wearing the coats he made for me. That indelible weight of an animal's skin on my skin—a weight of death.

Then: a handwritten copy onto a piece of 8.5 x 11 paper. (Most often I make several handwritten versions of a poem before I type it.)

Then: the first typed copy. Moving from the journal entry to that first typed version, I'd made only slight changes. "Once I could walk" became the more kinetic and symbolic, "Once I took a first step." The pelt's underside became "napped" to convey that texture, that touch of a processed pelt. And the hundreds of coats (hyperbole!) I later tried on? They had to be identified as women's coats, so the poem could show how outsized they were on my girl-body. The "terror of its beauty" became "that terrible beauty": more compact, more potent. I added an image to describe the act of putting each tried-on coat back onto the rack's metal bar. Still tethered to the quote that launched me into the poem, I titled these first drafts "Sacrifice."

Then: I went to work on that first typed version. "Sacrifice" became "Sacrificial." And even then I was uneasy with that title. As the poem pulled me closer into memory, "a first step" became "my first step." To better convey the image of little me with only my face showing above the bulk of that first fur coat, I tried "I'm all toddler-smile" rather than "I'm a toddler smile." "Fat" became the more precise "round," "Finish," became "end," its one syllable more decisive.

In the second stanza, I saw a different line break, one that gave me the line integrity of "outgrow that cony coat," a very appealing line, because it showcased assonance. And a few lines down, I saw I needed "later" to establish that I was older when I tried on the women's coats. I saw that "triptych mirror" would work, eliminating a preposition. "Dragging" (rather than "dragged") made the stanza end in a fragment. I liked the ongoing process a fragment conveyed.

In stanza three, "the animal's skin" became "an animal's skin." Again, I wanted to augment the sense of this poem's speaker having borne the weight of *many* animal skins. Here, nearing the end of the poem, it's easy to see me grappling with handwritten alternative ways to convey taking the fur coats off and hanging them up again.

This poem went through several subsequent versions. I thought about trying it in present tense. No, not good, because this poem needed to convey a process taking place over a number of years. I tried third person. No. It lost much of its immediacy in third person.

Eventually, I jettisoned the imagery about the snapshot, which detracted from the poem's "terrible beauty." That deletion then juxtaposed the grandfather and grandmother. Felicitous. "Ascended size" conveyed the physical sense of me growing up. "Women's coats" became "customers' coats" to better place the poem in the grandparents' fur shop.

And I named some of the furs. Ahhhhh . . . those animal names wield power. "Crawled into / an animal's skin" became "entered / an animal's skin," that new verb conveying much more than a merely physical invasion. I gave "Cool. Sleek. Gleaming" its own line, for spotlight. I indented and stair-stepped to give "I stroked / that terrible beauty" more surrounding white space, more silence to signal its import. "Weight" became "fallen weight." So much of this poem is about falling out of grace, falling into grace. "Hang" I left to hang at the end of a line. The next line, the penultimate line, then contained all one-syllable words, a way to slow the poem down before it reached its end. After a number of revisions, I changed the title to "A Furrier's Grandchild," a little workhorse of a title. Unpretentious, but worthy. And "Sacrificial" *did* seem pretentious.

The poem was published in the spring of 2021. But after its publication, reading it to an audience, I suddenly heard the poem convey to me another change. "I was reborn" became "I emerged. Reborn." My earlier revision (in which I changed "Each time I crawled into / an animal's skin" to "Each time I entered / an animal's skin") was signaling a different closure. The poem was saying, *First enter, then emerge transformed*. Above all, that's what a poem wants: to pull you in, to have you leave it transformed. The poem was offering me its magic, doing *its* revisionary work.

Oh, I'm an ardent believer in the rewards of revision. I do *not* believe in what I call the Myth of Divine Delivery, the notion that a first draft is the poem's one-and-only bonafide self, a gift from the Muse, thereby inviolable. Yes, it's true that Divine Delivery occasionally blesses most poets. A poem hits the page in almost finished form. A few strokes of fine-tuning, and it's as complete as it will ever be. But that—given my experience—happens rarely. When it does, I get down on my knees and thank the Muse. The rest of the time, I get to work and revise.

Revision. What an exhilarating, truly inspiring word! *To see again*. The fixedness, the seeming certainty of the poem in an initial version? This can be blinding. But revision offers to restore our sight. We ask the poem for fresh perspective, a new viewpoint. Leading us toward its true self, the poem lets us see what we could not see before. Revision, too, is a gift from the Muse. And to that, I say, Praise be.

CHAPTER 12
RADIANT ASSOCIATIONS
Philip Metres

Travel

I. Since I've arrived they've
grown. Outside, in

a country with no word
for outside, they line

the trees in red
bunches. I looked up

"ruby," toward "mountain
ash." There are

no mountains here
just these berries hidden

in the slow changing
leaves

II. we climbed the trees to pick
them, the leaves almost

as red. we scattered
half of them

on the ground, playing
games, so we could get them

into the other's clothes without
them knowing

First Draft:

Translation: A Bearing Across

I.
Since I've arrived, they've
grown. Outside, in

a country with no word
for outside, they line

the trees in red
bunches. I looked up

"rabina," found "mountain
ash." There are

no mountains here,
just these berries hidden

in the slow-changing
leaves.

II.
We climbed the trees to pick
them, the leaves almost

as red. We scattered
half of them

on the ground, playing
games, who could get them

into the other's clothes without
them knowing.

Wrist tired from grinding
The skins aside,

juices sugared twice,
my tongue almost stung

from its bitterness. Hot
teas eased the sting.

I remembered everyone
I loved and couldn't see.

III.
We worked hard last night
on just one line

of Triapkin's poem, trying to keep
the song with the snow: "Outside's

the snow, outside's the snow. October
12th, first

white wind rattling trunks. We'd
already lost

the fall.

IV.
This morning, the trees stand naked
of leaves. Just berries on long

black branches. They'll be here
all winter. My teacher.

said they sweeten with frost,
each snow a sugar. I know

tomorrow I'll bend down
the branches, feel

the cold on the backs
of fingers, pick

beautiful unnameables, think
of you, how something

in this world keeps
calling me back.

Final Draft:

Ashberries: Letters

1.
Outside, in a country with no word
for *outside*, they cluster on trees,

red bunches. I looked up
ryabina, found *mountain ash*. No

mountains here, just these berries
cradled in yellow leaves.

When I rise, you fall asleep. *We
barely know each other*, you said

on the phone last night. Today, sun brushes
the wall like an empty canvas, voices

from outside drift into this room. I can't
translate—my words, frostbitten

fingers. I tell no one, how your hands
ghost over my back, letters I hold.

2.
Reading children's stories by Tolstoy,
Alyosha traces his index

over the alphabet his mouth so easily
unlocks. Every happy word resembles

every other, every unhappy word's
unhappy in its own way. Like apartments

at dusk. Having taken a different street
from the station, I was lost in minutes.

How to say, where's the street like this,
not this? Keys I'd cut for years coaxed open

no pursed lips. How to say, blind terror?
Sprint, lungburn, useless tongue? How say

thank you, muscular Soviet worker, fading
on billboard, for pointing me the way?

3.
Alyosha and I climbed trees to pick berries, leaves
almost as red. On ladders, we scattered

half on the ground, playing who could get them
down the other's shirt without their knowing.

Morning, the family gone, I ground the berries
to skin, sugared sour juices twice.

Even in tea they burned. In the yard,
leafpiles of fire. Cigarettes between teeth,

the old dvorniks rake, scratch the earth,
try to rid it of some persistent itch.

I turn the dial, it drags my finger back.
When the phone at last connects to you, I hear

only my own voice, crackle of the line.
The rakes scratch, flames hiss and tower.

4.
This morning, the trees bare. Ashberries
on long black branches. Winter. My teacher

says they sweeten with frost, each snow
a sugar. Each day's dark grows darker,

and streets go still, widen, like ice over lakes,
and words come slow to every chapped mouth,

not just my own, having downed a little vodka
and then some tea. Tomorrow I'll bend down

branches, brittle with cold, pluck what I can't
yet name, then jar the pulp and save the stones.

What to say? Love, I live for the letters
I must wait to open. They bear across

this land, where I find myself at a loss—
each word a wintering seed.

Letters I Must Wait to Open

After graduating college, I traveled to Russia on a fellowship. I had proposed studying Russian poetry and its relationship to the fall of the Soviet Union, but in my heart I was going to Russia to learn how to be a poet. In Russia, I'd heard, poets were prophets, revered by the People and feared by the State. I'd fallen in love with the idea of Russia, but I wanted to see behind the mirror of my fantasy.

That's a good metaphor for the writing process—we fall in love with an idea, but we must travel past the fantasy and encounter the real. The journey of "Ashberries: Letters" over seven years and probably twenty drafts began in 1993, with a complete handwritten draft in my Russia notebook. I wanted to translate what I was seeing in the country around me—not only for myself, but for a beloved five thousand miles away.

The poem's journey was far longer than I could have imagined. In my twenties, I doggedly pursued poems, revising incessantly, but poetry kept sprinting ahead, eluding my grasp. I'd push the same words up the page, only to see them fall down. I saved at least fifteen versions of "Ashberries," nearly all of which show the patient critiques of my girlfriend and our writing groups. Most of the drafts show only modest changes—sharpening a phrase here and there. That slow unfolding was an agony for me, but I couldn't see what was missing.

Looking at the initial and final versions together, I am in awe of the process. A poet needs to maintain two opposing sensibilities: tenacity and curiosity, stubbornness and tenderness. Without tenacity and stubbornness, a poet drifts in the winds and whims of readerly desire. Without curiosity and tenderness, a poet cannot grow (and grow into) what the poem requires.

I abandoned the first title "Translations: A Bearing Across" because it seemed didactic and obvious ("translation" comes from Latin, to bear across). The second title, equally clunky, "Correspondences" captures the double translation of the poem—the speaker is wrestling with understanding the Russian world, but also trying to translate that reality for a distant love. The final title anchors the mysteries of translation in the humble ashberry tree, and the letters I'd send that tracked the progress of fall.

Lines got longer. While the first draft has a sparseness and minimalism in its lineation (a couple of lines have just one word), the second draft has a more regular line length and consistency through each of the sections. The reason? I'd fallen in love with the sonnet. Each of these sections are fourteeners, sonnets with irregular rhyme and meter. These are love poems to a person and to a country.

While I loved the couplets (for a poem about relationality and silence), I grew dissatisfied with the line breaks. The first version feels obvious, gratuitous, even forced, as in the opening:

Since I've arrived, they've
grown. Outside, in

a country with no word
for outside, they line

the trees in red
bunches.

While I see verve in the sharp enjambment, the choices don't feel particularly necessary, except for the one I kept: "a country with no word / for outside." Russian does have a word for "outside" but it's not a precise fit: a meteorologist might use the phrase "*na ulitse*"—literally "on the street." (I was the country with no words, not Russia!) While the line breaks of the final version do have some strongly enjambed lines, they move the reader in a more meditative, mysterious way.

The first draft contains moments of beauty, but the poem feels precious and inert. There's nothing yet of the love relationship that anchors the dislocated self in a dislocating world. By the final draft, all sections but the second weave the relationship into my struggle to connect and understand the world.

In addition, the first draft's use of "we" confuses a reader—who are these others with whom the speaker is plucking berries, making tea, and translating poems? In the final draft, there is no "we," only a beloved, Alyosha, my Russian "little brother," and a teacher. These relationships feel more grounded and emotionally specific.

In the first draft, the speaker's observations feel abstract. The stakes are not clear. I was trying to capture being enthralled by a country and by a person, then losing that initial spell and seeking what could help me endure a long winter alone. As I revised, I clarified the disorientation—and sometimes terror—of living in a distant country, and trying to navigate another language and culture without the people who love you.

That's why the late arrival of the second section felt like the turning point in my revision process when I recalled a time I got lost. The terror, the inability to communicate, and the (comic) relief of that section was my epiphany. Sometimes the most elemental and primal feelings that bring us to write something—those radiant associations that are most clear—take the longest to clothe in words. We know them deeply, and they frame everything we see, but our readers do not. Revision is seeing the poem as if we were someone entirely other.

Somehow I survived that winter. The letters I waited for, the wintering seeds, finally opened. And yes, reader, even before the poem was complete, we married. We keep finding each other.

CHAPTER 13
AN ACT OF FAITH
Abayomi Animashaun

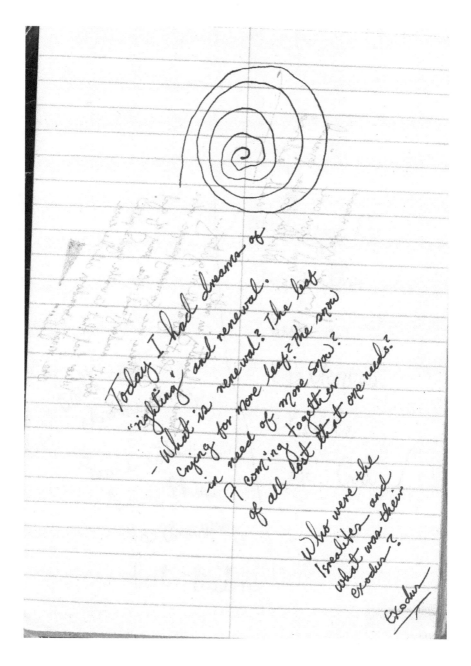

First Draft:

Exodus

Today I had dreams of "righting" and renewal.

What is renewal? The leaf crying for more leaf? The snow in need of more snow? A coming together of all lost that one needs?

Who were the Israelites and what was their exodus?

Exodus

Final Draft:

Exodus

When the last immigrants
Walked out of the gates

Fireworks lit up the sky
Horns and sirens blared

From every window
Flags draped

The country at last
Was itself again.

At the park, townsfolk
Celebrated *new liberation day* –

They cheered as foreign clothes
Were burned in piles

Danced when ethnic foods
Were flushed down sewers

And monuments to migrants
Were lassoed and pulled down

Including statues
Of the town's founders –

Immigrants some say
From the horn of Africa –

Whose clay heads now dangle
From a rope in the heart of town.

Discipline and Unknowing

Poetry for me is an act of faith.

Faith that by showing up to write (between the morning hours of three and six), I'll discover words and phrases beyond my limited imagination that sometimes become seeds for new poems or solutions for old unfinished poems.

I usually don't have an agenda when I show up each morning. I read a little. Rest in *unknowing.* Stare out the window, and idle in silence for a long time before finally putting pen to paper.

I never know where the writing will lead, but I accept the gift of each word, of each phrase, with the faith that each will yield in its own time as long as I continue to listen and remain steadfast.

To stay organized, I write in loosely held journals that are full of phrases, stick figures, and stray thoughts. Then, I return to the journal entries again and again (over the course of days, months, and sometimes years) to see how best to shape seeds into poems.

Here, for instance, is the journal entry (and process) that led to "Exodus":

Journal Entry –

> *Today I had dreams of "righting" and renewal.*
> *What is renewal? The leaf crying for more leaf? The snow in need of more snow? A coming together of all lost that one needs?*
> *Who were the Israelites and what was their exodus?*
>
> *Exodus*

*

When I stumbled on the word "Exodus", I *knew* I'd be writing about plagues and the Red Sea. But my poems seldom play out the way I see them initially. And when the lines of this poem began to appear, I found myself writing not about Moses, his laws, and his descent from Sinai, but about the poor treatment of immigrants in my own time:

Exodus

> *After the immigrants were gone*
> *The country was at last clean and right.*
> *The people felt this way*
> *Happy in their ways*

I didn't plan this. I'm not intelligent enough to predict how my loose writings will become poems. And, I'm still surprised by these first lines—written when children were being separated from parents at the US/Mexico border.

*

After writing those opening lines, I struggled. I couldn't hear the poem. It was unlike any I'd previously written. The tone seemed foreign. So I put it aside for weeks. I read other poets and worked on other poems. Yet, I couldn't abandon this new poem. I was drawn to its premise. Despite challenges, I felt if I stayed with the poem, my intuition would grow and merge with the poem's tone.

The breakthrough came when I was playing around with colors and adjectives. I tried "pink," "blue," "wary," "good," etc. None worked. All failed to open new doorways into the poem. But, when I tried "white," the poem took on new meaning:

Exodus

After the immigrants were gone
The country was at last white again
And clean and right. The people
felt this way. Happy in their ways

The tone had changed. Yet, I wasn't thinking of big issues at this stage. I was more concerned with finding room in the poem. And with that single word, the poem was no longer stalled. There was finally a path through it. Later that week, I added the following lines:

Exodus

After the immigrants were gone
Fireworks rang out in the night sky
From every window, flags draped

The country was at last white again
And clean and right. The white people
In the town felt this way

And they gathered at the park –
In chairs, on grass, on blankets –
To celebrate white liberation day

Feeling I'd made headway, I let this version sit for days.

*

Weeks later, when I read the poem again, I found this new version untrue and problematic. First, there are white immigrants. Second, the word "white" placed beside "liberation" in this manner is contrary to all I affirm.

Moreover, almost every white person I know took a stand against the poor treatment of immigrants during those difficult times—individuals, who said enough was enough, who maintained, in words and deeds, that immigrants are (as they've always been) vital contributors to the country's narrative. The word "white" did not belong in the poem.

Exodus

After the immigrants were gone
Fireworks rang out in the night sky
From every window, flags draped

The country was at last ~~white~~ (. . .) again
And clean and right. The ~~white~~ people
In the town felt this way

And they gathered at the park –
In chairs, on grass, on blankets –
To celebrate ~~white~~ liberation day

*

Elusive as this poem was, it was the ending that left me impatient. How does one close a poem about immigrants that unabashedly draws from the Old Testament? I couldn't end the poem with "French and Black immigrants" as seen in the following lines:

That night, the town's residents cheered
As ethnic books were burned in piles
And ethnic monuments were lassoed
Then pulled down, including the statues
Of French and Black immigrants

It felt clunky. False. But I knew I was close. So I kept showing up. I refused to lose faith in my process. The poem had taken on life. It was almost formed. I couldn't force it into my prior notions of what it could have been by referencing Moses' adoptive mother, who drew him out of the river, gave him his name, and raised him in Pharaoh's house. I had to follow the poem down another river, one that slowly emerged from the act of writing, to a conclusion I read now and marvel at still.

CHAPTER 14

REMOVING DETAIL
Tami Haaland

I follow the trail
through a sea of sagebrush
two butterflies leading me.
Pennyroyal (I think) the
quick hop of a jerusalem
cricket & I'm thinking
of Leslie Marmon Silko's
Yellow Woman. That man
could come up anytime
w/ a horse. and we could
go into the high mountains
higher thunder. Later
I might come return.

This is a good frontispiece horse?

First Draft:

Deer on Crazy Creek

The way you held your head, ambling along the trail
The sway of your body, a look of contemplation
All internal, two feet in front of the other two
Not thinking or thoughts wandering
As alone as I had been moments before you appeared
One moment before you saw me too three miles
Into Crazy Creek Trail, long patches of sage brush
Intermittent aspen and pine. I sat on a huge
Split boulder, heavily lichened, speaking to stone.
All along the trail I thought how risky the venture,
But not risky, the signs that say don't go it alone
Into bear country, into this high mountain country.
I can see miles except in the aspens. Going uphill
In sage I think of Yellow Woman, of the stranger
Who finds her and takes her into an other life.
For a moment I dream of a man on a horse, perfect
Environment, I think, for him to ride up and offer.
It's after that, after another grove of aspen
I climb on the rock and then see you, deer woman
Following the path your people probably made
Long before humans thought they should manage
And map this place. You are doing what we do,
Head down, step ahead, step ahead. Neither of us
So alone in this creek as we thought, and when you
Lift your head and I begin to speak to you
For a moment you stop and decide and
For a moment I wonder what you think of
Before you see me. Does your mind swirl around
Your own grown children, the possible bear
At the edge of the mind, the long trail ahead
The golden butterflies in the sage, the small
Flies that nag the flesh, and in the distance
The flicker bird that calls, then calls again
From the aspen horizon.

Final Draft:

Deer on Crazy Creek

Along the trail I think how risky the venture,
the signs that say don't go alone into bear country.
I can see miles except in aspen. Walking uphill
in sage I think of Yellow Woman, of the stranger
who finds her and takes her into another life.
It's after that, after coming from a grove of trees,
I climb on a huge split boulder and watch
an ant navigate a forest of lichens. When I
raise my eyes to the horizon, I see you,
the way you hold your head, ambling
along the trail, the sway of your body on this
path made long before humans managed and
mapped this place. You are doing what we do:
head down, step ahead, step ahead.
When you look up and I begin to speak, you stop,
deciding whether to bolt or continue, a turn
for us both. I wonder, do your thoughts go
to the bear at the edge of the mind, the long trail
with golden butterflies on sage, flies that chase
and bite? Do you understand what calls
and calls again from an aspen horizon?

Making the Local Exact

"Deer on Crazy Creek" began one July day on the Beartooth Plateau in Montana. The earliest lines came while I rested on a granite boulder split in half, maybe from lightning, maybe from millennia of freezing and thawing. Sitting on that boulder, I began my notes: "I follow the trail through a sea of sagebrush." Later I committed these words to the typed page and came up with the first version of the poem without a title. This draft has thirty-four lines compared to twenty-one lines in the final version.

In the process of revising, I eliminated poet and friend Julian Stannard, who served as the voice of skepticism in my original notes. This early version begins directly with the deer instead of the setting, but it presumes too much. For example, "a look of contemplation / All internal" is unnecessary, and so that passage doesn't make it into the final poem. Similarly, I cut "Not thinking or thoughts wandering" because the speaker doesn't need to speculate about the deer's thoughts. In the original moment, I was aware of one female creature encountering another, and I wasn't worried about the internal makeup of the deer. I simply recognized her dailiness, her relaxed gait, and signs of fatigue. The question, as she approached, was whether she would bolt or be willing to go past me on the trail. This question creates tension in the poem, and I chose to focus on this moment by eliminating unnecessary details.

I mention Crazy Creek Trail on line seven of the first draft, which I quickly changed. The title, "Deer on Crazy Creek" eliminates the need for explanation and gives the poem a clear location from the start. While the boulder remains, the idea of "speaking to stone" disappears because it sounds too mystical. Yet this location is a central resting place in the poem and serves as a microcosm of the larger environment, with both colors and textures reflected in the surrounding landscape.

Because this poem takes place in an area where "don't go alone into bear country" signs are posted at every trailhead, it was easy to incorporate that sentence into the poem. The fact of bears in the environment brings risk to the poem and amplifies the importance of seeing "miles except in aspen." That's why these lines remain in subsequent versions as a characteristic of the place.

In fact, when I was walking this trail that led to the initial notes, I thought of Leslie Marmon Silko's well-known story called "Yellow Woman." Remote areas have a timeless quality, and myth does not seem out of the question. But to go into detail about the story didn't serve the progression of the poem. I also edited out the return to the "deer woman" image. However, the idea of a trail originating either with humans or animals serves the poem by blurring boundaries just before the woman and the deer meet.

In the final poem, everything depends upon the deer's decision and the questions that follow. The woman and the deer have their routines—"head down, step ahead, step ahead." From this point, most of the first version remains in the final poem with some modification. I removed the grown children, but I kept the "bear at the edge of the mind," though the syntax is perhaps a too obvious allusion to Stevens, because it implies a danger that does not materialize and thus represents awareness that could lapse into worry. I kept the beauty of the "golden butterflies on sage," which apparently may have been white according to my earlier notes. They are juxtaposed with "flies that chase and bite." The original word is "nag," but horseflies in the wilderness do, in fact, chase and bite, and the deer would have been bothered by the flies as much as the human.

In the final sentence, following a suggestion from poet Sandra Alcosser, I removed the specific reference to a red-shafted flicker. In this landscape, aspens appear on the horizon, and it's from those trees the unnamed voice emerges and persists at the end of the poem. Though I know the flicker call well, it was better if this speaker does not have a name for it. Instead, she is taken with its mystery, "what calls / and calls again from an aspen horizon."

This account of revision makes the decisions seem easy and quick. Some were. For example, moving location into the title happened almost as soon as I started revising, but such a shift can be an obvious first step in the process. The more comprehensive revision comes more slowly, less consciously, and often because readers—fellow writers and trusted collaborators—point out what I may have overlooked. The crucial work of giving and getting feedback is an essential practice of a writing life, and then the poet is left with choices to contemplate that lead, ultimately, to the finished poem.

CHAPTER 15
FORGING SOMETHING NEW
Charles Finn

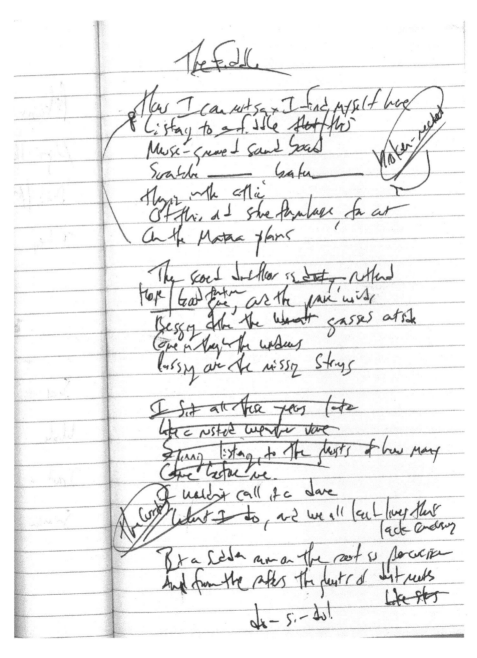

First Draft:

The Fiddle

Far out on the Montana plains
How I cannot say I find myself here
Listening to ~~a that~~ this fiddle   *broken-necked*
mouse-gnawed soundboard
scratched _____, broken _____
hanging in the attic
of this old stone farmhouse, far out
on the Montana plains.

The scored dirt floor is ~~dirty,~~ rutted
Hope/Good fortune _____ gone, and the prairie winds
begging at the ~~wheat~~ grasses outside.
come in through windows
passing over the missing strings.

~~I sit all these years later~~
~~Like a rusted weather vane~~
~~Spinning, listening, to the ghosts of how many~~
~~Come before me~~.
I wouldn't call it a dance exactly
the curtains   what ~~I do~~, and we all <u>live lives that lack conclusions</u>
but a sudden rain on the roof is percussion
and from the rafters the ghosts of dust motes ~~like stars~~   *(do-si-do)*
come down to ~~settle on my shoulders~~. *Granted*
~~Granted~~, I'm ~~may~~ be here on a fool's errand
where memory's anvil rusts in the corner
with nothing to forge, but deep in the wonder
and embedded shadows that inhabit us ~~all~~
I swear I hear that fiddle sing.

Final Draft:

Memory's Anvil

Somewhere far, far out
On the Montana plains
Left in the attic
Of an old stone farmhouse
Hangs a broken-necked fiddle
With mouse-gnawed soundboard
And missing strings.

I hear it most nights.

The scored dirt floor below
Is rutted, the footsteps gone
There's less and less
For the walls to be concerned about
To say nothing of the wind
Come all these miles.

Nor would I call it a dance exactly
What the faded curtains get up to
But we all live lives that beg ambition
And I'll wager they're doing their best
Like the unexpected rain on the roof
A welcome percussion, and the dust
That comes down from the rafters
To do-si-do.

Oh how I like to lie awake and listen
Cry a little if truth be told
Imagining the tunes that fiddle played
When the music of bare feet and thigh slap
Accompanied it, fighting off drought
And golf ball hail, filling this old house
Not a little unlike prayer.

The Winch of Imagination

I'll be the first to admit I write bad poems. You could almost say I have a knack for it. But I like to keep them, those false starts and lackluster endings, the fruitless middles, because I know I can always go back and try to make them better—which I do. I make them better by making them worse, and then a little better, and then a little worse, and then a little better. It's like rocking a car out of a snowbank. Then I give up. It's obvious I'm going nowhere, buried my poem up to its axles in a rut of language I can't get out of. But I'm still not done. Because in a week or month or year, there I am again, attaching the winch of my imagination to give another pull.

Like many poets, I don't produce a series of stand-alone drafts. I revise constantly as I go. Revision, in fact, is my favorite part of writing. The tinkering and changing, going over and over the same line again and again until the exact right word presents itself and the music of the poem is seamless.

What I'm calling my first draft here is really just the first quick thoughts that got the poem going. In the case of "Memory's Anvil" I was re-reading *All But the Waltz*, by Mary Clearman Blew, a poetic memoir about growing up in rural Montana. Halfway through, Blew mentions a fiddle with "mouse-gnawed soundboard" hanging in the attic of an old stone farmhouse.

On line nine you can see where I filled in the blank I'd initially left before "gone," first trying "hope" and then "good fortune," but quickly rejecting both as too vague, trying too hard to be deep and meaningful, too blatantly "poetic." On line seventeen, I swapped "settle on my shoulders" for the more western and active "do-si-do" which I found echoed nicely with the line from above: "I wouldn't call it a dance exactly." Almost immediately, the four lines in the center of the poem beginning "I sit all these years later," I crossed out, realizing that they added nothing. All these changes came in the first couple of passes before I moved to the computer and uncountable changes that followed.

The most obvious change I made is to the opening. Instead of beginning with the clunky "How I cannot say I find myself here," I felt the reader should know right away where the poem takes place. In this case it was easy to move "Far out on the Montana plains" to become the first line, but the problem was it was still flat, without music. My solution was to insert "Somewhere" and add a second "far" to create the more floating "Somewhere far, far out / On the Montana plains."

Obviously, the poem turns on line eight with "I hear it most nights," referring to the fiddle. In the first draft that line doesn't exist, instead I'm listening to the (not yet broken) fiddle in line two. But by switching to describe the broken fiddle first, then reveal later I can hear it, the surprise is much more potent. In addition, deep into the revision process, line eight ended the first stanza, but every time I read it, it seemed to lack punch. The obvious solution? Set it off on its own, thus giving it more impact.

Much of the middle part of the poem I saved but reconfigured, reading it out loud until the cadence of the words fit together. That said, as the drafts progressed, I wanted the interior of the poem to "clang" (like a hammer hitting an anvil) and so from the first draft to the final, I clipped the lines, making them much shorter. I liked the syncopation the enjambment produced.

I also liked the idea from the first draft: "We all live lives that lack conclusion." This, I felt, is where the poem began to say something. But each time I read it, the phrase ever so slightly tripped me up. Over the years, I've learned to listen to this inner voice and eventually "beg ambition" (which suggests yearning) replaced "lack conclusion" (which leans toward failure and sadness). Another pet phrase I jettisoned was "a fool's errand." Again, I liked the idea it hinted at, and in revision wrote many lines around it, but was this memory really a fool's errand? On closer examination, I didn't think so, and so took it out.

The last stanza is completely new. Not a word can be traced back to the first draft. All I can say is as I wrote and rewrote, revision showed me the hole in the poem, allowing me to imagine the tunes the fiddle played. Through rewriting, I discovered the poem wasn't about a broken fiddle or even the "shadows that inhabit us," but the *life* that was lived in that farmhouse.

Finally, the title. I always leave it to last. As I tested different titles in my head and on the page, the phrase "memory's anvil" from the first draft kept nagging at me. I contemplated saving it for a different poem, but since this poem revolves around memory, and a rusted anvil is just the type of thing you often come across on these old homesteads, it finally occurred to me it made an appropriate title. After all, the poem describes a homestead, a place where memories are forged, beaten into shape. Titles need to do the same.

Ultimately, for me, revision isn't about addition and subtraction, but lateral thinking and creation, taking the raw material of inspiration and passing it through the furnace of experience—and, with any luck, forging it into something entirely new.

CHAPTER 16
MAINTAINING FIDELITY

Shin Yu Pai

First Draft:

> *for as long as I am able*

The Empty
    ~~Empty~~ Zendo

    In the second year.   *the*
         finding your ~~my teacher~~ gone   *grass hut*
of ~~your absence~~
I sit ~~alone~~ in my backyard
cottage alone, during   *keeping safe*
during the corona pandemic
the sangha divided now
across time, lives, and borders
we are ~~and~~ brought together
     on our laptop computers

Final Draft:

Empty Zendo

(for Bill Scheffel)

when is the hall never not vacant?

alone in my cottage
I think of my teacher

gone now two years

straining to hear
the sound of the inverted bell,

a Tibetan bowl sings,

while I study the interiors
of other human habitations

transmitted over computer cams,
the sangha divided now,

more than ever, I will practice
for as long as I am able

Emptying the Zendo

My poems don't typically undergo heavy revision. I reformat a piece to give it shape, symmetry, or uniformity. More substantive reimagining arises out of wanting to clarify a particular point, or to create depth and complexity to make the poem ring out. I edit for anything that feels too much like prose. But mostly, I'm interested in maintaining a fidelity to a feeling or image. And it's this image-feeling upon which my poems turn.

"Empty Zendo" opens my most recent poetry collection *Virga*. Written during quarantine, the poem contemplates the act of spiritual practice following the loss of a spiritual teacher. I wanted the poem to evoke the sense of acute isolation during the Covid-19 pandemic, juxtaposed alongside the solitary nature of practice, even within the context of larger community, or *sangha*.

In my first draft, I highlighted the absence of the teacher to allow loss to permeate the poem. I imagined the lineage of meditators and the places where they practiced alone—grass huts, caves, rooms, and meditation halls—in contrast to my own modern backyard cottage. I wanted to directly reference the moment in which we are all living, which led me to specifically call out the pandemic and coronavirus. I felt that bringing in aspects of technological innovation, like Zoom conferencing, could be an era-specific marker and contrast to the simplicity of sitting in community together. Early versions of the title included "The Empty Zendo," "For As Long As I Am Able," and "Pandemic Meditation."

As the poem evolved, I wanted to be less direct in stating facts. In the final version, I let the title "Empty Zendo" do the work to set the tone. Philosophically speaking, even when a meditation hall or zendo is filled with bodies, one can think of the zendo as empty. Empty of egos, empty of mind, empty of identity. The title also conjures an image of the zendo as being abandoned and disused. I cut the article from the title to compress the language and to make the syllables more rhythmic in their recitation.

Instead of opening the poem with a memory of my teacher, I began the poem with a koan to invoke the mental space of practice. I made this choice to depersonalize the context to more quickly and effectively invite the reader into the poem. The question that is directed towards the reader becomes "when is the hall never not vacant?" It is with this invitation to enter the poem and to contemplate together that I then move through the context of vacancy. Rather than invoking the abstractions of time and space travel, I focused on the physical details and sensations of practicing together over computer cams. I chose details that could bring the reader into the room and activate their senses with auditory and visual cues, through both listening and looking. To reinforce the sense of doubled meaning, I referred to "the sangha divided now"—to suggest both the literal cleaving of the community caused by the pandemic and to also set up subsequent poems in *Virga* which refer to spiritual and creative betrayals that led to deep fractures in the community. Revision occurs not just within the context of the poem, but within the context of my larger projects.

I brought the draft title "for as long as I am able" into the poem's closing. It's this phrase that gives meaning to the act of contemplation. Whether the speaker practices alone, or in community, ultimately, she is alone and without a teacher. She must rely upon herself to define her own relationship and commitment to practice. Like a vow that is renewed every day, that commitment is unwavering even as, simultaneously, the language of the poem suggests that it has its limits. I chose to move from the more omnipresent point of view presented by the opening of the poem to a direct perspective, to actually deploy the personal "I" to take it out of the philosophical space and into a lived experience.

The shape that I arrive at is a poem structured into couplets and single lines. Organized by units of thought and pause between images, the poem is conversation with itself. A soliloquy where anything overstated—like the nature of a division itself—is stripped out. I like the idea of beginning a poem with a question, which in this instance I chose to respond to obliquely. Faced with a puzzle, I answer the question by choosing to not answer it at all, to break the koan's logic. Revision, for me, is like polishing a gem to bring out its beauty. However, that working and reworking of the stone also changes its rawest qualities and alters its energy. The place where I decide to put down the pen and stop fussing with the poem is not the place that another poet, teacher, or scholar might choose to end. Ultimately, we find our own relationship to our voice and our objects through reading, practice, and deep listening. In this way, we are each our own teachers.

SECTION IV
"I ASKED MY DREAMS"

CHAPTER 17
WHAT'S AT STAKE
Kim Stafford

31 December 2020

End of a tough year. What will it take in us to make the next better? Woke at 1:30 and lay long worrying about Guthrie in the snow—losing his way back in falling white. Must give him whistle, phone, flashlight, and down coat. "Walk all night around a tree."

In life, we are on guard all day, worshipping safety and comfort. In art, we seek to get lost in a land of dangers, wonders, and enigmas.

Lost in Snow

When all day falling the white sky
has covered every track back
to the road for home, and turning
you see every tree is like every tree
in the circumference of camouflage,
and your recognition dawns at dusk
that you are lost for the night,
choose a hemlock or a fir
that gives some shelter, and
with your left glove touch
the trunk as you walk around
your spindle of certainty,

counting as you circle the circuits,
knowing if you wander you
are doomed, if you sleep
you are gone.

First Draft:

Lost in Snow

When all day falling the white sky
has covered every track back
to the road for home, and turning
you see every tree is like every tree
in the circumference of camouflage,
and ~~your~~ recognition dawns at dusk
that you are lost for the night,
choose a hemlock or a fir
that gives some shelter, and
with your left glove touch
the trunk as you walk around
your spindle of certainty,
counting if you like the circuits
knowing if you wander you
are doomed, if you sleep
you are gone.

Final Draft:

Lost in Snow

When all day falling the white sky fills
every track back to the road for home, when
turning you see every tree is every tree
in their blank circumference of camouflage,
when no matter how you swivel you can't find
your way, when recognition dawns at dusk you are
lost for the night, there is nothing for it now, you
must choose a hemlock or a fir that gives shelter,
a trunk with no low limb to impede your journey,
and with your left glove on the rough dim bark
begin to walk around your certain spindle, counting
if you like your circuits one hundred, two, then three,
or counting breaths that puff more palpable as cold
deepens and the dark drifts closer, knowing if you
wander you are doomed, if you sleep you are gone,
but tramping endless circles will convey you
safe to sunrise.
                              So by grief
you say his name softly to yourself as you orbit
the vacant place he was to be dizzy with it, you say
his syllables through the dark hours, through changing
moons around and around in place, but not going deeper
into the dark wood where no one could find you.
Oh precious tree, plain companion, root and anchor.

Getting More Intimate With Pain

This poem evolved in response to external need and internal discovery. I first scribbled "Lost in Snow" the morning our son was to ski Oregon's Mt. Hood, where conditions were bad. I wrote to remember what to tell him if a storm struck. But then, first draft done, it was still early, before dawn, and there was time before I would talk with him, so I tinkered with the poem, adding details of cold, darkness, snow, the puff of the survivor's breath, and the long circling journey around the tree to sunrise.

We had our talk, he headed for the mountain, and I turned to other tasks . . . but I kept coming back to the poem. I remembered Richard Hugo's advice about "writing off the subject" in his book *The Triggering Town*. I realized the poem needed something to make the snow matter. Often, revision begins for me by asking the first draft, "So what? So . . . this happened—why is that important? What's at stake, deeper, really?"

This was shortly after Barry Lopez had died, and his family was much on my mind. As I thought about Barry's wife, Debra Gwartney, I realized she would be lost, too. What do you do, in grief, to not stagger deeper into sorrow? Haunted by Debra's need from outside the poem, I went into revision by adding a second stanza, where the cold was grief, the snow was mystery, and the landmark, the tree, must be some kind of survival snubbing post for anyone adrift in sorrow.

I often find the first draft has a kind of kindling genius, an instinct for a first subject . . . but in revision the second genius sparks, a recognition that the first subject is insufficient, and lightning has to strike again somewhere inside the text. I thought back to my own tragedies—especially the death of my older brother, by suicide, thirty-three years ago. I remembered how some feral instinct got me to get life going again. How could I summon that into the poem?

The word "dizzy" entered the draft, then "the dark hours," then "moon," then "dark wood." I wanted a poem studded with sensations. I remembered Ellen Bass once saying a poem is not about an experience—a poem is an experience. The second part of the poem, the turn into the dark wood of human grief, became the real poem. And if that was the real poem, then my first stanza had to rise in service as preamble. The word music of "dizzy" and "dark wood" could be anticipated by adding phrases like "no low limb" and "rough dim bark" and "safe to sunrise." I realized revision begins by finding what words worked best, then letting those effects summon further elements that weren't yet there. As I typed version after version, I watched individual lines grow, as the first draft's "every tree / in the circumference of camouflage" became "in the circumference of utter camouflage," which became "in the blank circumference of camouflage." The forest started to crowd the speaker, and I loved that mounting claustrophobia. I wanted to get this character, the speaker in the poem, in trouble.

The process of revision for me is like looking at a painting: you step back to see the whole canvas, then come close to see how the brush strokes create effects. In and out, far and near, whole concept and then the textured scent of word, syllable, letter.

Paradoxically, once the forest became a metaphor for grief, I needed to strengthen that effect by insisting on the physical reality of the place itself: "No ideas but in things."

And, as always, needing to tighten the language, I made a sweep to eliminate extra words and syllables: "spindle of certainty" became "certain spindle"; "no lower limb" became "no low limb"...

But then how to end it? Like the lost traveler, I turned to address the tree itself with a feral cry: "O precious tree, plain companion, root, and anchor." Typing that, I wept for my brother, and for Barry ... for Debra. The poem had become more than words. It was a shovel to excavate.

When I look back over successive drafts, I see my effort was to get more intimate with pain, with snow, with the forest, to go deeper into fear and cold and enigma. As I wrote, details gathered around the poem's predicament. It wasn't so much a matter of changing words, the surface, but of changing my psychic location from desk to forest, from writer to participant in the action the poem summons. I needed to get inside what the poem shows, look around that interior, and pull in words that speak precisely for that place. First, to get inside the snowy grief of dusk ... and then recruit words to enact the pang of being there.

Once I felt the poem becoming real as an experience, I could attend to words again, the surface. I saw the chance for effects like "no low limb" and then "limb ... dim." Then little events of alliteration like "certain spindle," "dark drifts," "safe to sunrise." Then to whispered passages like "say his name softly to yourself," "say / his syllables," and the percussive "not going deeper into the dark wood ..."

Revision, for me, begins in asking a first draft, *What are you really about? What's at stake here? Why does this matter? What is my inner life trying to tell me by foregrounding these first words on the page? What's under them, beyond them, eager to be revealed?*

The poem becomes my guide, and I obey its needs by seeking to make it more like what it wants to be.

CHAPTER 18
ZEROING IN ON INTENT
Prageeta Sharma

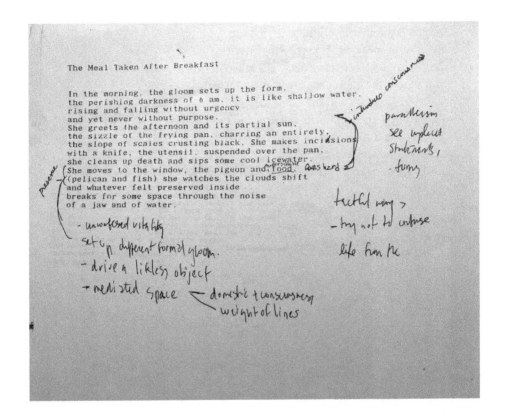

First Draft:

The Meal Taken After Breakfast

In the morning, the gloom set up the form.
the perishing darkness of 6 am, it is like shallow water
rising and falling without urgency
and yet never without purpose
she greets the afternoon and its partial sun,
the sizzle of the frying pan, charring an entirety,
the slope of scales crusting black, she makes the incisions
with a knife, the utensil, suspended over the pan.
she cleans up death and sips some icewater.
She moved to the window, the pigeon and food
(pelican and fish) she watches the clouds shift
and whatever felt preserved inside
breaks for some space through the noise
of a law of water.

Final Draft:

The Witness
after Rilke

She greets the afternoon and its partial sun as would a corpse.
A cheerless day inspires a restless sound. Without meaning to go,
as habit creates meaning, she counsels the fish on the stovetop.
She makes incisions with a knife. It was a cheap feeling:
If her magnificence only awakened the ashamed was what she to do?
There is no time to envision opulence or a brazen country,
to carry on with nocturnal affairs, amass the arms folded underneath
fallen trees, it is too quiet for you. Therefore her body became the next victim
after that, all had to become inaccurate or pretended: Desire had fallen wayside.

The Poem's Psychic Center

What do we do with the poem that changes so dramatically from the first draft to the final that it resembles almost nothing from the original? Is it still the same poem? What if the practices that ultimately change it are drawn from a conceptual lens, maybe thematic, and based less on syntax and more on a revision zeroing in on intent?

For me, revision is about retaining and deepening the original sentiments intended for a poem. I found the original version of "The Witness" (at the time titled "The Meal Taken After Breakfast") in a folder of poems I saved from my first graduate workshop in 1993 at Brown University. This draft had already undergone a serious overhaul and considers my workshop feedback—written in my hand—and comments from my professor Marjorie Welish, who tended to offer stylistic and conceptual frameworks for reading rather than build revision from rewriting, editing, or correcting syntax. In the case of "The Witness" I had not yet found the buoying and spirit of articulation needed, but the feedback/notes helped solidify ideas I wanted and that I learned in the time between writing the first and second draft. (Mind you, I realize there were grammar edits that needed fixing in my original draft—lots of run-ons and non-standardized English—it was a messy first draft.) All this I want the reader to keep in mind as I address the conceptual revisionist practices that contributed to the writing but can not be seen in my drafts.

For me, revision is also about answering a set of questions, making use of what the poem sets out to be, and fleshing out what I began when I wrote the first draft. For example, what does it mean to transform a poem to its themes and keep very little of it? What is the poem's intention? If I recall, the exercise was to consider how Rilke managed to write about events that never made it into a poem, that were somehow both "outside" and "inside" the poem, yet served as a kind of psychic center. I wanted to describe something where an image wasn't built in the poem, rather outside of it, and the effect of its presence in creating a new central theme for the poem.

As you can see, the language in the first draft is more descriptive than the second. What I realized with the first draft is I wanted to bring description to a place where the images could speak to an emotional condition. I needed to add more self-reflection to the poem and maybe interrupt the description like Rilke does. (The obvious example is "The Archaic Torso of Apollo" but you can find it in so many of his poems.) I also wanted to infuse my poem with more phenomenological aims that might invite a new tone, thus creating the psychic center I was after and move away from stark realism.

The title changes the discourse of the poem, but not its intent. To me, "The Meal Taken After Breakfast" sits slovenly in the domestic, whereas "The Witness" immediately invites a new vantage point. I would say that the moves initiated in the first poem lapsed into descriptive writing without an idea of deepening the flow of lineation. I notice my notes want me to will more "consciousness" into the poem. The second line and dangling simile seemed messy to me. How could the poem embody this simile rather than landing on a distant simile? What stays is how the speaker moves, thinks, observes, and becomes the singular witness of the poem, one that is about making lunch, cleaning a fish, and observing an object that she wants imbued with life, like herself on a "cheerless day." But I saw how the poem needed to steady itself in how this "she" wanted to greet the day rather than staying submerged solely in a domestic act of cooking.

Rather than fixing anything, I tried to inhabit what the marginalia suggested. I recall Welish asking me to create a mediated space of "domesticity" and "consciousness. She asked what could the weight of my lines hold, in the way of Rilke? How do I "drive a lifeless object" into the next draft and think through "unconfessed vitality" so that the poem was less confusing and didn't rely so heavily on description to emote? What were the strategies here? The lines that change the poem for me are: "She makes incisions with a knife. It was a cheap feeling: / If her magnificence only awakened the ashamed what was she to do? / There is no time to envision opulence or a brazen country . . ." The poem wants to witness the restless figure whose desires go beyond her domestic scene and this is what the revised poem accomplishes.

CHAPTER 19
IN THICK DARKNESS WE LISTEN
Shann Ray

* * *
whole poems,
yes punctuations,
no capitalization
lo nt God

3 POEM CYCLE
(O GOD OF MY FEAR)
(O GOD OF MY DUNGS

①

O GOD OF my ABANDONMENT

THE WELL OF GOD

WHEN I WAS A BOY
MY FATHER PERFORMED WHAT I THOUGHT TO BE
TO BE UGLY WORK WITH HIS HANDS.

HE REMOVED TICS THE SIZE OF GARLIC CLOVES,
FROM THE BODY OF OUR BIRD DOG
A FEMALE WHO GAZED
DROPPING THEM EACH ONE LIKE DARK COINS
INTO A BUCKET OF GASOLINE.

HE PUT DEER HEADS SKULLS IN A BARREL
OF MAGGOTS UNTIL THE SKULLS WERE LICKED CLEAN
AND HE SET THEM ON THE ROOF FOR THE DEATHER TO WHITEN.
OF OUR THE SCHULE WORE AT THE WEATHER WORE DESOLATE.
BEFORE THEY BECAME BEAUTIFUL THEY BECAME DESOLATE.
HE SHOOK MY BROTHER IN THE CAGE

OF HIS HANDS SO THE BONES WENT BAD WORD

& THE FACE WELLED
AND I LOOKED ON AS A FOOL LOOKS ON

DESASTER, WE NEVER KNEW LOVE,

MY BROTHER & ME I UNTIL WE WANDERED
AND FOUND AND OURSELVES AT OUR FATHER'S
CRYING,
BEDSIDE, NOW, CUPPING OUR FACES IN HIS HANDS, CRYING,
KISSING & KISSING US, ON THE CHEEK,
KISSING & KISSING US, ON THE CHEEK.

maggie too loud
75% enjambment
25% end stopped
for her sweet spot
* see LOVE ENDINGS
handout
+ ENJAMBMENT
AS THE CONTEMPORARY
MEAN?
MORE OPEN
THAN CLOSED
ENDED SENTENCES
& STANZAS

HOW CAN I
RE-VISION?
MOVE LINES
AROUND
TO GIVE
THEM
BEST
PLACEMENT,
BEST
LINE & POEM
POWER.

First Draft:

God of my abandonment

o God of my abandonment
~~the will of God~~
when I was a boy
my father performed what i thought to be
ugly work with his hands.

he removed tics the size of garlic cloves,
from the body of our bird dog
~~a female who gazed~~
dropping ~~each one~~ them like dark coins
into a bucket of gasoline.

he put deer heads in a barrel
of maggots until the skulls were licked clean
~~so he could~~ and he set them on the roof
of our single wide for the weather to whiten.

before they were beautiful they ~~became~~ were desolate.
he shook my brother in the cage
of his hands so the bones went ~~bad~~ wild
and the face welled w/
and i looked on as a fool looks on

disaster. we never knew love,
my brother and ~~me~~ i, until we grew old
and found ~~and finding~~ ~~filled~~ ourselves at our father's
bedside, him crying/cupping our faces in his hands, laying
~~kissing and kissing us, tenderly, on the cheek~~.
kissing and kissing us.

Final Draft:

God of my abandonment

Montana Triptych

1 / God of my abandonment

when i was a boy
my father performed what i thought to be
ugly work with his hands

from the body of our old bird dog
he removed tics the size of garlic cloves
dropping them like dark coins
into a bucket of gasoline

he put deer heads in a barrel of maggots
until the skulls were licked clean
and he set them on the roof of our singlewide
for the weather to whiten
before they were beautiful they were desolate

he shook my brother in the cage
of his hands so the bones went
and the face welled
and i looked on as a fool looks on
disaster we never knew love
my brother and i until we grew old
and found ourselves at our father's bedside
him holding our faces in his hands
kissing us and kissing us

Obscuring a Formidable Power

God dwells in the thick darkness.

This ancient avowal, mysterious as it is physical, drew me to the original making of my poem "God of my abandonment." In this poem, I question equally God as light or God as love informing and reconstituting darkness. Paired with the fundamental beauty of light, it seems to me dark matter and gravity are at work when poets create and revise poems.

This poem was originally titled "The Well of God." I discarded that title, not liking the allusion to 'the will of God.' One can also see in the marginalia of the original draft a nascent focus on line endings and on people held or beheld by love in the context of personal and global atrocity. My own Czech bloodline's silencing and erasure during WW2 at the site of the Lidice massacre outside Prague, and the nature of family then to now, informs my revision work.

*

I was raised in the high mountains and broad plains of Montana. My father was fathered by men who were hunters and trappers, so my brother and I share a strange inner world familiar with skull and horn, the eye teeth of elk, bear claws, the jawbones of small animals, a magpie's tail feathers, the notch of color at the shoulder of a red-winged blackbird. As a boy, I felt bodily what came to the mind later in life, and in poetry I began to see the body—the body of the world, of wilderness, of people—as a vessel to bear unavoidable and unaccounted trauma, as well as a vessel of fusion, one capable of healing, reconciliation, restoration, and atomically speaking, resurrection in its universal adherence with light across time, space, and being.

Einstein said, "There are two ways to live your life. One is as though nothing is a miracle. The other is as though everything is a miracle. God is subtle but not malicious. The most beautiful thing we can experience is the mysterious—it is the source of all true art and science." Einstein's "miracle" informs the revisions for "God of my abandonment."

*

When naming the world, we obscure a formidable power in whatever we choose to name. The word "eagle" can give an impression that we know the essence of the creature, but nature declares we should hold more dread and awe. The body of *aquila chrysaetos*—a raptor whose wingspan reaches eight feet, whose grip generates 400 pounds of pressure per square inch, whose eye sees a hare from three miles away—disturbed the poem and my revisions. Felt beneath the surface, the eagle, or in this case the mystery, goes unnamed in this poem, creating an invisible updraft through which it moves.

During revising, my goal was to reveal, if obliquely, the unseen. For instance, the reader will notice all words except "God" forego their power of capitalization, receding in the attempt to more humbly encounter "God." The line "from the body . . ." is switched with the line "he removed tics . . ." in affinity with how the mystery moves within trauma toward healing. A single poem (see the upper margin) becomes a series of three poems including "God of my fear" and "God of my illness." The "O" of each of these titles is dropped for less sentimentality and more direct call and response. The words "a female who gazed" are cut for being a too direct replacement of the White supremacist patriarchal gaze that haunts world trauma, while the things themselves in the poem represent the feminine nature of God in the ancient Christian prayer called the "Anima Christi," one which takes the feminine form in the Latin, and the feminine form in the unseen or the silence below the poem. The Jesuit notion "God in all things" complicates the poem, and "each one" becomes "them" for quickening. The word "skulls" becomes "heads" for better cadence and also to allow "skulls" to stand alone later. Line endings loosely follow Maggie Smith's 75%/25% directive from the right margin. The phrase "so he gazed" is cut for the same reason as "a female who gazed" above. Small word choices are cut or changed for rhythm, alliteration, and precision. For example, "bad" and "wild" are cut, so "went" can present a more formidable, less melodramatic construction. The same for "crying" and "cupping," as well as "kissing and kissing" in order to more readily carry the intimacy assumed in fatherhood (aligned with and confused by the parable of the prodigal) and primordial understandings of what it may mean to be "children of God."

In my poetry, I fear I cross nature and diminish our collective love and power by trying too rationally to name the unknown. But I also believe, with Pythagoras, that because of physical truths and metaphysical understandings we might attempt through art and science to see into the music of the divine and poetic order of the universe. Revising for me is very much like that music, the music of water and how in the wilderness water shapes rock, how water enfolds the body, cleanses us from within, invites us into relationship. As water unifies and refracts light, revision is both intricacy and expansiveness. Have you ever seen the bird of which I speak—loyal, carnivorous, alight behind you arcing skyward or moving at great speed low over the river, dipping a talon through water clear as glass, a reflection the eye might receive at a glance or perhaps never catch? Revision is mystery. By brushing up against it in the dark, by seeking to name the unnamable, we might make of our words something humble and ineffable. In the thick darkness I hear weft of wing upon updraft. I hear the down-sweep of the unseeable. As I walk the Beartooth Range in southeast Montana with my loved ones, I walk toward the place where darkness becomes dawn.

In the thick darkness, if we listen, we may hear a voice whisper . . . *arise.*

CHAPTER 20
THE SERPENTINE PATH
Todd Davis

The fish windows through
the water. Light furrows
the waves at the base of
the falls. The cave in the
valley whose limestone
floor disguises the river
when it worms underground
has drawings on the walls.
In one a bear stands
with arms in a Y, reaching
toward the sun. In another
a bear sleeps beneath a
tree the color of a tamarack
in November. In another
a bear walks toward the
center of a circle, innocent
of the bodies eaten.
Ursus stands in the half light,
places paws on wall and squints.
These fish, the way they rise,
porpoise, bodies flung like
garments in wind, sweeping

muscle attached, bent and bound,
lengthened flat beneath fur or
skin, along the jaw, the neck,
the skull, down the neck,
working in concert so Ursus can
tear, can chew, can grind, and swallow.

back and forth in the
currents. He wishes the dead
man, the dead woman, the dead
hand who etched visions
onto stone, might draw
a brook that in late fall,
spawning colors, the sun's
fire at dawn, the sky a hundred
writhing blue tentacles.

First Draft:

Ursus in the Cave

A fish windows through
water while light furrows the waves
at the base of the falls. The cave
in the valley whose limestone
floor disguises the river
when it worms underground
has drawings on the walls.

In one a bear stands with arms
in a Y, reaching toward the sun.
In another a bear sleeps beneath
a tree the color of a tamarack
in November. In yet another
a bear lumbers toward the center
of a circle, innocent of the bodies
he's eaten.

Ursus stands in the half-light,
places paws on the wall and squints.
Those fish, the way they porpoise,
bodies flung like garments in wind,
muscle bent and bound, lengthened
flat beneath fur or skin, along the jaw,
the neck, the skull, working in concert
so Ursus can tear, can chew, can grind
and swallow.

Final Draft:

Tributary

*I learned to catch the trout's
moon whisper.* — Hart Crane

Fish window
water, rise
to bugs
that flock
the air.

Disguised
by limestone
the river worms
underground.

In darkness
on walls
drawings
thousands
of years old:

A bear stands
with arms
reaching
toward
sun.

A bear sleeps
beneath
tamarack
the color
of November.

A bear couples
with its
mate, head
nuzzled
to neck.

In the absence
of light
Ursus squints,
uses a nail
to sketch
the fish
he hopes
to catch.

Like water,
muscle shifts
across time:

The dead
hand
that etched
the first
rock.

A bear's claw
that draws
the trout.

The hidden moon
the trout
whispers to
before
disappearing
into stone.

Following a Tributary to Find a Poem

"Tributary" is a poem I drafted quickly while writing my seventh book *Coffin Honey*. I never returned to it, and it didn't make its way into the final manuscript. Like many of my poems, this one appeared while I followed a thread, a line of association and narrative fragment. Like water moving down the mountain where I live, the poem flowed along gravity's course, creating a water gap, making a path to follow.

After I publish a new book of poems, before I retire the journal or notebook I used while writing that book, I spend a few days reading back over, seeing if I overlooked any lines or early drafts. Often something that struck me as stale or flat in the past shines with a different illumination.

I had no plans to continue to write about Ursus, a bear-figure who must navigate the encroaching human world. But as I went back through my notebook, I found a passage I wrote in November 2018. Reading those early scribbles three years later, I was drawn to the scene, following Ursus in the dark of a cave, his discovery of images on the damp walls, his hunger for meaning-making (and my own!) and for a very real fish to eat.

In the first typed draft, I included a title to situate the reader, "Ursus in the Cave," and then began to play with line breaks and stanzas. I eliminated some language while transcribing it from my notebook, particularly near the end of the poem—words like "sweeping," "attached," "down the neck." I wanted greater compression for two reasons: a more meditative space and an understated dynamism.

As I read the first draft aloud, I wasn't as interested in Ursus's innocence as a predator—"of the bodies he's eaten"—or in the ways he can tear, chew, grind, and swallow the prey he's hunted and killed. While bears are marvelously made, I'd written other poems that focused on this aspect.

With that insight, perhaps the most crucial and altering step occurred. Sometimes forces exterior to a poem will lead to a significant revision, and that was the case here. A poet friend wrote to me during this period about the petroglyphs in the Susquehanna River. That was it! The drawings of past peoples, of people who lived in a place for thousands of years, their desire to represent their experience in art, that was the deep pull I'd felt reading over that older journal entry. My mind wandered to those petroglyphs and other cave paintings I've gazed upon. Here was a space trout could swim in, where Ursus could hunt, a space I could make in a poem, the words sliding around the stones of my teeth.

The final piece in this shift involved the epigraph. Later in the same journal, I discovered a line by Hart Crane I'd copied down: "I learned to catch the trout's moon whisper." As a lover of trout, especially native trout like cutthroat or brookies, I've tended to collect phrases and passages that conjure these fish. But I puzzled over Crane's line. To my knowledge, Crane was not an avid angler, nor did he have any special knowledge of trout.

Yet the line lured me. What is "the trout's moon whisper"? Would Urus recognize it when he heard it? Could it be conjured in a poem? The moon controls some of the formal constructions of the earth, like the tides, and it's responsible for many cycles.

Flora and fauna of all sorts, humans included, find themselves drawn to it, physically and spiritually.

And with that in mind, a conversation began between my poem and the line from Crane's poem. I decided to depart radically from the original three-stanza form and ended up creating a poem of eleven stanzas, placed in two columns, side-by-side, like images on a cave wall. I shortened the line length considerably, often allowing only two or three beats, to better represent the compressed nature of cave art, the skeletal, stick-like quality of some of those drawings. Where once I'd written "limestone / floor disguises the river / when it worms underground," in the final draft the image is far more succinct: "Disguised / by limestone / the river worms / underground."

I did not wish to forsake clarity or the individual moments of narrative each drawing presented. I wanted to connect Ursus to place—the idea that those who'd made the drawings had a deep relationship with Ursus's ancestors. Thus, the focus on noun–verb construction in the fourth, fifth, and sixth stanzas: "A bear stands," "A bear sleeps," "A bear couples." In the final draft, Ursus's agency became more pronounced. He adds to the drawings in the cave, becoming not just a subject of the art but a creator of it: "Ursus squints, / uses a nail / to sketch / the fish / he hopes / to catch."

I often tinker more consciously with the music of a poem in final drafts, an acknowledgment of the symbiosis of sound and sense. After the examination of the petroglyphs depicting the lives of past bears, the poem's urgency increases. To accentuate this, I enhanced the rhyme and consonance with closer echoes: sketch, catch, etch, claw, draws. And as the poem slowed toward mystery, I lengthened the words, accentuating the assonance in the long vowels that pull at the ear and mind: moon, trout, stone.

Most days I follow tributaries across the mountain of my home, hiking from the seep where a tributary begins to where it connects to another tributary, and finally to the river in the valley. The key to revision for me is to keep testing language, following it toward the overlooked connections between ideas, narratives, and images. I must allow myself to be surprised by its serpentine path in the same way I'm surprised by the lives I find living in the water and in the woods around it. The forest of language, the home of all poems, offers this very delight and surprise.

CHAPTER 21
DREAMING POETRY
Beth Piatote

② ③

was not a language or a season // but colonization
of a mother tongue, another tongue way still
~~our~~ ~~but~~ ~~but~~ words like love, graft
and seed, ~~so we don't forget but~~
bring, ~~and~~ [rather ~~than toss~~] is ~~multiplication~~
~~say~~ ~~even~~ in barren days bring [proliferation].
we ~~bet~~ ~~we still~~ not barrenness but
on ~~it~~ ~~know~~
Recall ~~the~~ root ~~of~~ is few / "fish," not winter, and ask
= course quiet
what [depths] of ~~stillness~~ may we find, if we sway
like fish to deepest water, ~~bring~~ suspend
~~rest~~ ~~fold~~ ~~comfort of~~ ~~best intuitence,~~
effort, reaction. ~~Draw the body down.~~
~~multip~~ Become only heart, and essence.

~~To survive the bitter of~~ behave
When ~~surface light and~~ warmth recedes, ~~of~~ follow sage

~~That you may survive~~
~~There is not teaching in hiber~~
~~The fish who is your teacher~~
~~Safe is the darkness~~
~~Survival comes in~~
~~Trust the dark of ness of it~~
~~Go So you may survive. So you may be safe.~~
Become Still as ~~fish~~ [the word unspoken], that ~~you may~~ stay

Alive

First Draft:

Hibernation

[sonnet]

> hiléew'ce – it is (still) in winter
> (e.g. fish) is resting in deep water
> *Nez Perce Dictionary* 351

Nestled in the ~~word for blanket folds~~ curves of hibernate is *hiber*
Latin for winter, cousin to *l'hiver*, a word
I learned to please my ~~partner's~~ mother-in-law, who lived
in France, though Moroccan. What we shared

was not language or season but colonization
of mother tongue ~~another tongue~~ Still words like ~~war~~ love graft
and seed, ~~so we don't forget but~~ and [~~rather than loss~~] give ~~even in barren days~~
~~we bed we sow~~ bring not barrenness but ~~multiplication~~ proliferation
Recall ~~the~~ our root ~~of~~ is ~~lew~~ *fish*, not winter, and ask

What ~~depths~~ course of ~~stillness~~ quiet may we find, if we sway
Like fish to rest in deepest water, ~~bring~~ suspend
Effort, reaction. ~~Draw the body down~~ Become only heart, and essence

~~To survive the bitter of~~
~~when surface light and warmth recedes, follow sage behave~~

~~that you may survive~~
~~there is no teaching in hiber~~
~~the fish who is your teacher~~
~~safe is the darkness~~
~~survival comes in~~
~~trust the darkness of w~~
~~go so you may survive so you may be safe~~
~~become still as fish~~ [~~the word unspoken~~] ~~that you may stay~~

Alive

Final Draft:

Because our Roots are in Rivers, Not Latin

hiléew'ce – it is (still) in winter
(e.g. fish) is resting in deep water[1]

Consider this translation:

Not that winter
is the root of hibernation
but that rest
the stillness of fish
is the root
of hibernation.

hiléew'ce
fish rests in deep water

To speak the language of rivers
to survive winter's cold

hiléew'ce

become fish, and move
toward darkness, muscle away
from light
and ice

sway
to rest
in deepest water, suspend
effort, reaction.

Become only heart, and essence.

---

[1]léew' *v.* 1) to be winter, 2) to hibernate. Possibly léew *fish* and 'i *v. to lie, lie down, be lying down* (*Nez Perce Dictionary* 351; 1005–6)

How to Not Write a Sonnet

My poetry notebooks are basically disordered lists of poems I'd like to write. Sometimes these are poem ideas, fragments of images, poem titles, or distillations of feeling. And sometimes they are poem forms, with notes on syllable, rhyme, or subject rules, or commentary on a great poem I just read. There are pages of my notebook that have poem drafts, and others that are mostly blank or aspirational, that may just say "sonnet" or "villanelle" at the top with a few notes, hoping that the right content for the form will arrive and then magic will happen, like the shoemaker and his elves.

I am working with a particular constraint—or rather, a particular font of possibility— in my poetry: to illuminate the grammar, beauty, and ontological brilliance of my Indigenous language, Niimiipuutímt/Nez Perce. My goal is to use poetry for Indigenous language revitalization, and this means crafting bilingual poems that will assist language learners in grasping Nez Perce grammar and usage, while also offering lovely, accessible gems of observation for general readers. In the case of "Because our Roots are in Rivers, Not Latin," my goal was to write a sonnet that illuminated the word *hiléew'ce*, literally, "fish lies (still)," which is a Nez Perce word for hibernation.

To begin, I reviewed sonnets by Shakespeare and my notes on form. I started drafting by hand, and soon lines of language, devotion, and winter's cold appeared. I felt optimistic that the poem could join themes of historical and personal intimacies with the thought-world specificity of *hiléew'ce*. I liked two lines that made a near rhyme with "suspend" and "essence" and I decided to use them for the final couplet. But even with all this promise, I was three lines short.

As I looked at the hole in the stanza I began to have doubts about the direction of the poem. I texted a poet friend (always good to have around) and wrote: *I'm three lines short of a sonnet, which sounds like a euphemism for insanity but in this case is my actual problem.* He suggested that I write three words, one on each line, as guides. Later he asked if I was intentionally writing a sonnet or if it just appeared that way.

Looking back, his question struck at the core of my revision process, because a writer is both responsible for craft (making intentional decisions) and for attunement to the organic form of the poem (allowing the poem to be what it wants). I wasn't sure whether the sonnet form was right for this subject. Both form and content—to the extent that they can be separated—were not working. Following the advice of generations of writers before me, I decided to *go outside*. I took the dog for a walk and ruminated; I invited my body and my mind to move freely. There were too many ideas in the poem, and not enough words.

I considered whether the stall was a problem of form, and whether the sonnet structure was impeding the optimal expression of the poem.

I needed to distill what the poem was really about, so I asked my dreams to help me. This strategy was another version of going for a walk; I had to shake things up. I needed to access a deeper level of my creativity that was not yet flowing through my pen, to go somewhere with the poem where I wasn't in control of it but simply able to observe and learn from it. In most cases this work can be done in waking life. But when we write, we are free to use every resource we have available, and in this case I asked my dreams to help me understand the soul of the poem.

That night, I dreamed that I saw a snowshoe rabbit near a stand of low bare brush on a snowy hillside. I was looking out at the snow from the perspective of the rabbit. In the morning I wrote two pages in my journal about how to survive in winter. I decided to preserve these fragments: *What language winter speaks / when rabbit translates his coat to say: I am snow.*

The dream brought out this theme: winter translates us, and animals remind us to embody this translation and not resist it.

If the poem were to be true to the subject, to *hiléew'ce*, then it had to move at a slower pace. It had to embody the language not only of Niimiipuutímtki but the language of winter. Hibernation's idiom is slowing down, going deep, getting rest. Snowshoe rabbit turns white to survive on the surface; the fish rest in the river's slowest groove. The sonnet, while perfect for nature and love and multitudes of subjects, was moving at too fast a pace to arrive in a place of stillness. A conventional sonnet is written in rows of iambic feet, a pattern that lopes along at a clip, then offers up a pithy volta at the end: ta-da! I needed a slower form.

In my revision, I aimed for a form that would imitate the movement of fish and would create a sense of spaciousness and stillness. I also stripped down the themes to language and survival. I retained several of the original lines of the sonnet, and repurposed the first line from the sonnet into the title, "Because our Roots are in Rivers, Not Latin."

The best way to not write a sonnet is to try to write a sonnet, knowing that all words, lines, and forms are provisional. Trust your instincts about what brought you to get the words on the page, and as you revise, offer every resource you have—other poets, walks outside, dreams, writing and rewriting—to discover what the poem wants to be. Give your whole self to the process.

CONTRIBUTORS

Abayomi Animashaun is an immigrant from Nigeria. He is the author of three poetry collections and editor of three anthologies. A winner of the Hudson Prize and a recipient of a grant from the International Center for Writing and Translation, Animashaun is an assistant professor of English at the University of Wisconsin, Oshkosh and a poetry editor at *The Comstock Review*.

Jimmy Santiago Baca is the author of thirty books, films, and documentaries. His latest book is a poetry volume, *No Enemies*, by Arte Publico Press, University of Houston. He lives in New Mexico with his family.

Todd Davis is the author of seven books of poetry, most recently *Coffin Honey* (2022) and *Native Species* (2019). His writing has won the Foreword INDIES Book of the Year Bronze and Silver Awards, the Midwest Book Award, the Gwendolyn Brooks Poetry Prize, the Chautauqua Editors Prize, and the Bloomsburg University Book Prize. He teaches environmental studies at Pennsylvania State University's Altoona College.

Charles Finn is the author of the nonfiction collection *Wild Delicate Seconds: 29 Wildlife Encounters*, and in collaboration with photographer Barbara Michelman, author of *On a Benediction of Wind: Poems and Photographs*. His essays, poems, and fiction have appeared in a wide variety of journals, magazines, and newspapers across the United States. He lives in Havre, MT with his wife Joyce Mphande-Finn and their cat Lutsa.

CMarie Fuhrman is the author of *Camped Beneath the Dam: Poems* (2020) and co-editor of *Native Voices: Indigenous Poetry, Craft, and Conversations* (2019). She has published or forthcoming poetry and nonfiction in multiple journals, including *Emergence Magazine, Platform Review, Yellow Medicine Review, Poetry Northwest,* and several anthologies. CMarie is a regular columnist for the *Inlander*, translations editor for Broadsided Press, and nonfiction editor of *High Desert Journal*. CMarie is the director of the Elk River Writers Workshop and director of poetry at Western Colorado University, where she also teaches nature writing. She is the current Idaho Writer in Residence. She resides in the mountains of West Central Idaho with her partner Caleb and their dogs Carhartt and Cisco.

Tami Haaland is the author of three poetry collections, including *What Does Not Return* and *Breath in Every Room*, a Nicholas Roerich First Book Award winner reissued by Red Hen Press in 2021. Her poems have appeared in *Ascent, Consequence, The American Journal of Poetry, basalt, The Ecopoetry Anthology,* and *Healing the Divide* among other publications and have been featured on *The Writer's Almanac, Verse Daily, American Life* *in Poetry*, and *The Slowdown*. Haaland is a former Montana Poet Laureate, a recipient of the Montana Governor's Humanities Award and Montana Artist Innovation Award. She was one of many artists who collaborated with UK filmmaker Anna Cady on her *Elemental Dialogue* series. Haaland teaches at Montana State University Billings.

Yona Harvey's poetry books are *You Don't Have to Go to Mars for Love*, winner of *The Believer* Book Award in Poetry, and *Hemming the Water*, winner of the Kate Tufts Discovery Award. Her poems have appeared in *Obsidian: Literature & Arts in the African Diaspora*, *The Best American Poetry*, *Letters to the Future: Black Women/Radical Writing*, and *A Poet's Craft: A Comprehensive Guide to Making and Sharing Your Poetry*. She co-wrote Marvel's *World of Wakanda*, a companion series to the bestselling *Black Panther* comic, and co-wrote Marvel's *Black Panther & the Crew*.

Jane Hirshfield is the author of *The Asking: New & Selected Poems* (fall, 2023). Earlier books include *Ledger* (2020), *The Beauty* (2015), long-listed for the National Book Award, and *Given Sugar, Given Salt* (2001), a finalist for the National Book Critics Circle Award. Other honors include fellowships from the Guggenheim and Rockefeller foundations and the National Endowment for the Arts. Her work appears in *The New Yorker*, *The Atlantic*, *The New York Times*, *The TLS*, *Poetry*, and ten editions of *The Best American Poetry*. A former Chancellor of the Academy of American Poets, she was elected in 2019 into the American Academy of Arts & Sciences.

Rose McLarney's collections of poems are *Forage* and *Its Day Being Gone*, winner of the National Poetry Series, and *The Always Broken Plates of Mountains*. She is co-editor of *A Literary Field Guide to Southern Appalachia* and *Southern Humanities Review*. Rose has received fellowships from MacDowell, Bread Loaf, and Sewanee, among other awards. Her writing has appeared in publications such as *Kenyon Review*, *New England Review*, *American Poetry Review*, *Prairie Schooner*, and *Southern Review*. Her fourth book is forthcoming from Penguin. Rose is an associate professor at Auburn University.

Philip Metres is the author of ten books, including *Shrapnel Maps* (2020), *The Sound of Listening: Poetry as Refuge and Resistance* (2018), *Pictures at an Exhibition* (2016), *Sand Opera* (2015), *I Burned at the Feast: Selected Poems of Arseny Tarkovsky* (2015), and others. His work has garnered the Guggenheim Fellowship, the Lannan Fellowship, two NEAs, seven Ohio Arts Council grants, the Hunt Prize, the Adrienne Rich Award, three Arab American Book Awards, and the Cleveland Arts Prize. He is professor of English and director of the Peace, Justice, and Human Rights program at John Carroll University and core faculty at Vermont College of Fine Arts.

Naomi Shihab Nye is a Palestinian-American writer, editor, and educator who is on faculty at Texas State University. She grew up in Ferguson, Missouri, Jerusalem, and San Antonio, Texas, and has been a visiting writer in hundreds of schools and communities all over the world. She has written or edited more than thirty books of poetry, novels for teens, picture books, essays, and short fiction, including *Sitti's Secrets*, *Habibi*, *This Same Sky*, and *The Tiny Journalist*. *19 Varieties of Gazelle: Poems of the Middle East* was a finalist for the National Book Award. *The Turtle of Oman* and *The Turtle of Michigan* are novels for children.

Shin Yu Pai is the author of *Virga, ENSŌ, Sightings, AUX ARCS, Adamantine,* and *Equivalence.* She served as Poet Laureate of the city of Redmond from 2015 to 2017. In 2014, she was nominated for a Stranger Genius Award in Literature. She is a three-time fellow of MacDowell and has also been in residence at Taipei Artist Village, the Ragdale Foundation, Centrum, and the National Park Service. Her poetry films have screened at the Zebra Poetry Festival and the Northwest Film Forum's Cadence video poetry festival.

Paulann Petersen, Oregon Poet Laureate Emerita, has seven full-length books of poetry, most recently *One Small Sun*, from Salmon Poetry in Ireland. A Stegner Fellow at Stanford University, she received the 2006 Holbrook Award from Oregon Literary Arts. In 2013 she was Willamette Writers' Distinguished Northwest Writer. The Latvian composer Eriks Esenvalds chose a poem from her book *The Voluptuary* as the lyric for a choral composition that is now part of the repertoire of the choir of Trinity College, Cambridge, UK.

Beth Piatote is a writer of fiction, poetry, essays, plays, and scholarly works. Her 2019 mixed-genre collection, *The Beadworkers: Stories*, was longlisted for the Aspen Words Literary Prize and the PEN/Bingham Prize for Debut Short Story Collection, and shortlisted for the California Independent Booksellers "Golden Poppy" Award for Fiction. Her play, *Antíkoni*, was selected for the 2020 Festival of New Plays by Native Voices at the Autry. She is Nez Perce, enrolled with the Confederated Tribes of the Colville Reservation, and a founding member of luk'upsíimey/North Star Collective, a group of Nez Perce writers and language activists. She is an associate professor of English and comparative literature at the University of California, Berkeley.

Sean Prentiss is an associate professor at Norwich University. He is the author of *Finding Abbey: The Search for Edward Abbey and His Hidden Desert Grave*, which won the National Outdoor Book Award, and *Crosscut: Poems.* He is the co-author of two textbooks, *Environmental and Nature Writing* and *Advanced Creative Nonfiction*, and co-editor of *The Far Edges of the Fourth Genre: Explorations in Creative Nonfiction* and *The Science of Story: The Brain Behind Creative Nonfiction.* He and his family live on a small lake in northern Vermont.

Shann Ray is the author of nine books of poetry, fiction, and creative nonfiction, including *Atomic Theory 7* and *American Masculine.* Professor of Leadership Studies at Gonzaga University, he has led engagements with the Cheyenne Nation, Stanford, Princeton Theological Seminary, and the United Nations. His work has been featured in *Poetry, Esquire, Narrative*, and *McSweeney's.* The recipient of the American Book Award, three High Plains Book Awards, a National Endowment for the Arts Fellowship, and a Western Writers of America Award, he has served as a visiting scholar of leadership, forgiveness, and genocide studies in Africa, Asia, Europe, and the Americas.

Prageeta Sharma is the author of *Grief Sequence*, among other works. She is the founder of Thinking Its Presence, an interdisciplinary conference on race, creative writing, and artistic and aesthetic practices. She is the Henry G. Lee '37 Professor of English at Pomona College.

Kim Stafford has taught for forty years at Lewis & Clark College, where he is the founding director of the Northwest Writing Institute. His dozen books of poetry and prose include *Having Everything Right: Essays of Place*; *Early Morning: Remembering My Father, William Stafford*; and *The Muses Among Us: Eloquent Listening and Other Pleasures of the Writer's Craft*. He has taught writing at many schools, and in Mexico, Italy, Scotland, and Bhutan. In 2018 he was selected by Oregon's governor as Oregon Poet Laureate for a two-year term. He lives in Portland, Oregon, with his wife and children.

Frank X Walker is the first African American writer to be named Kentucky Poet Laureate. Walker has published eleven collections of poetry, including his most recent, *Masked Man, Black: Pandemic & Protest Poems*, and *Turn Me Loose: The Unghosting of Medgar Evers*, which was awarded the 2014 NAACP Image Award for Poetry and the Black Caucus American Library Association Honor Award for Poetry. Voted one of the most creative professors in the South, Walker coined the term "Affrilachia" and co-founded the Affrilachian Poets. He serves as Professor of English and African American and Africana Studies at the University of Kentucky.

Joe Wilkins directs the creative writing program at Linfield University, where he is a professor of English and environmental studies. He is the author of a novel, *Fall Back Down When I Die*, praised as "remarkable and unforgettable" in a starred review at Booklist. A finalist for the First Novel Award and the Pacific Northwest Book Award, *Fall Back Down When I Die* won the High Plains Book Award. Wilkins is also the author of a memoir, *The Mountain and the Fathers* and four collections of poetry, including *Thieve* and *When We Were Birds*, winner of the Oregon Book Award.

Terry Tempest Williams is a writer, educator, and activist. She is the author of more than twenty books including the environmental literature classic, *Refuge: An Unnatural History of Family and Place*; *Leap*; *Red: Patience and Passion in the Desert*; *The Open Space of Democracy*; *Finding Beauty in a Broken World*; *When Women We're Birds*; *The Hour of Land: A Personal Topography of America's National Parks* and most recently *Erosion: Essays of Undoing*. She is currently writer-in-residence at the Harvard Divinity School. Her writing has appeared in *The New Yorker*, *The New York Times*, *Audubon*, and *Orion Magazine*, and translated around the world. A member of the American Academy of Arts & Letters, she divides her time with her husband Brooke between Castle Valley, Utah and Cambridge, Massachusetts.

INDEX

Names of writers cited are in *italic*.